RECIPES THAT MAKE YOUR TASTE BUDS DANCE & YOUR BODY, TOO.

Serving You
LIFE

TANJIE BREWER

Mention of specific companies, organizations, or authorities in this book does not imply endorsement by the author or publisher, nor does mention of specific companies, organizations, or authorities imply that they endorse this book, its author, or the publisher.

Internet addresses, telephone numbers, names and titles given in this book were accurate at the time it went to press.

Copyright © 2020 Tanjie Brewer

All rights reserved. No part of this publication may be reproduced or transmitted in any form or by any means, electronic or mechanical, including photocopying, recording, or any other information storage and retrieval system, without the written permission of the publisher.

While all attempts have been made to verify information provided in this book and its ancillary materials, neither the author nor publisher assumes any responsibility for errors, inaccuracies or omissions. Any slights of people or organizations are unintentional.

The purpose of this book is to educate and entertain. The author or publisher does not guarantee that anyone following the ideas, tips, suggestions, techniques or strategies will become successful. The author and publisher shall assume no liability or responsibility to anyone with respect to any loss or damage caused, or alleged to be caused, directly or indirectly, by the information contained in this book.

Cover and Layout Design by aspiretodesign.com

ISBN: 9780578837963

Printed in the United Stated of America

THIS COOKBOOK IS DEDICATED TO THOSE WHO BELIEVE THEY HAVE A PURPOSE TO FULFILL AND NEED MORE ENERGY TO ROCK IT. TO EVERYONE THAT WANTS TO SERVE THE WORLD AROUND THEM ON A GREATER LEVEL, LET THIS COOKBOOK NOT ONLY SERVE YOU A PLETHORA OF NEW FUELING RECIPES BUT MORE ABUNDANT LIFE.

"MAY THIS COOKBOOK CAUSE EACH OF YOU TO STAND STRONGER IN *beautiful strength.*"

Table of Contents

Introduction 7
Getting Started..8
Give Thanks 19
Breakfast 20
Mid-Morning Meals 36
Soup 48
Lunch 56
Mid-Afternoon Meals 76
Dinner 86
Sides 102
A Sweet Delight 144
Sit, Sip & Savor 162
Schedule It Out 176

Your PLATE should support your MANDATE. I define your mandate as your purpose. We all have been commissioned to serve the world with our talents and gifts in some capacity. I believe that we all have a signature purpose that no one else can fulfill but us. Maybe you are a stay at home mom or dad, an entrepreneur, a police officer, a nurse, or a teacher, take a moment to think about what your purpose requires? How much of you, your time, and most importantly your energy does being the best in that area need? Many will agree that it requires a lot of energy to rise to the occasion of excellence daily. I often hear that in the morning, energy levels start off fairly high and for some, that happens after their first cup of coffee. Now answer this, what is your energy level like at the beginning of the day compared to the end? Are you able to sustain your vibrancy all day? This cookbook is meant to serve you a bit of life so you can serve the world on a greater level.

YOUR *Plate* & YOUR *Mandate* GO HAND IN HAND.

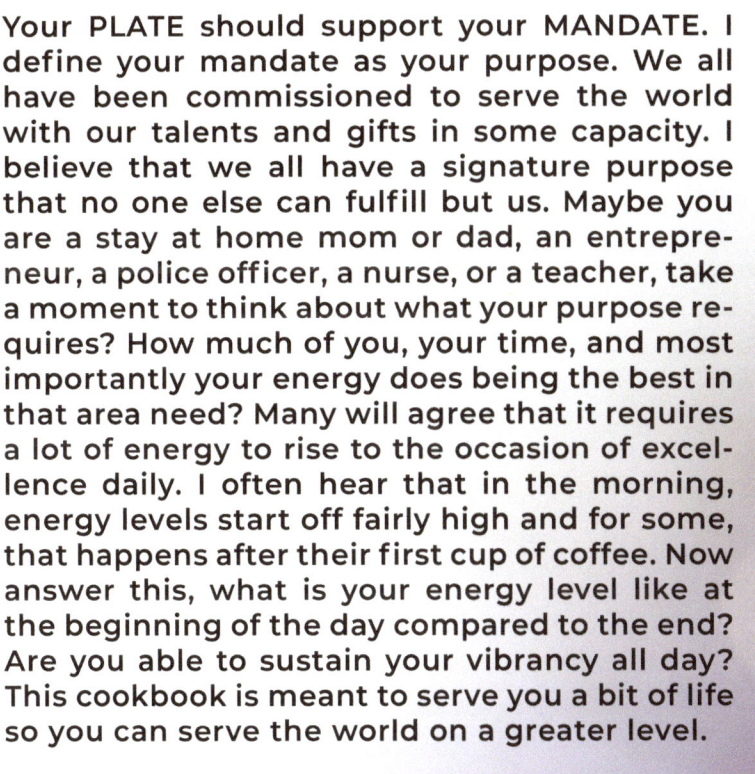

The Energy Factor

If your energy is not as high as you would like or your body is not where it needs to be, take a look at what your fork is currently serving you. Everytime food enters your mouth, it sends a message to your body. That message tells the body what nutrients are about to be served. Sometimes the messages are not always what the body wants to hear. You're either serving energy or your energy is being depleted. On a scale of 1 to 10, 10 being the best, how would you rate your energy level for the entire day? Regardless of your score, everyone will benefit with increased energy by implementing what you read in this book.

I've lived a vegan lifestyle for over thirteen years. I made this decision because I realized that eating live food vs. processed food made an energy deposit. I've always been told that my energy is through the roof. Of course, exercise and the proper thoughts help, but I realized that what I chose to eat was truly the deciding factor for my energy on any given day. Once you realize that food is energy, you become more conscious of what you eat. I wanted to share my message with the world, so I created the Lifestyle of Vitality challenge which is responsible for transforming countless bodies and lives around the world. Through my expertise in nutrition and exercise, I will continue to empower others to make wellness a lifestyle.

It's Beyond Vegan. It's Vivacious!

I chose to present you with a cookbook that many will consider as "vegan recipes". Vegan simply means a diet excluding meat or dairy products. Some may explore this lifestyle for health benefits, because of their desire to support animals, or because it is the "it" thing. I want you to remove ALL labels when taking a journey through this cookbook. Think beyond plant-based, vegan, or vegetarian. Though there are benefits of them all, I want you to think VIVACIOUS. My desire is to simply serve you life filled recipes that will revitalize your body. Eating live foods that are minimally processed are exploding with benefits to keep your amazing body thriving. As you view each recipe, you'll see what some of those benefits are. The purpose of this book is not to turn you against meat or dairy, but to add more life to your dinner table by serving you nutrient dense dishes. Furthermore, these dishes will help to increase the alkaline environment of your body. Keep reading, you'll find out more about acidic vs. alkaline.

> **"IF YOUR ENERGY IS NOT AS HIGH AS YOU WANT IT TO BE, TAKE A LOOK AT WHAT YOUR FORK IS CURRENTLY SERVING YOU."**

Why Alkaline?

The environment of your body matters!

It's very important to know that all food is not created equal. After you consume certain foods, they will either leave an acid or alkaline ash in the body. This means if you eat more foods that leave an acidic ash, it makes your blood acid, and eating a variety of foods that leave an alkaline ash, makes your blood alkaline. Why is this important? It's important because the environment of our body matters. The goal is that your body is alkaline with a pH of about 7.4. This is achieved by ensuring we eat meals that have an 80% alkaline to 20% acidic ratio. Studies have shown that disease has a harder chance of surviving in an alkaline body. It's when the body becomes acidic that illness is said to become more prevalent. Below is a list of examples of both alkaline and acidic foods.

(SHINE WITH ALKALINE) ASH FOODS

This category should reflect 80% of your plate at meal time.

Almonds	Lettuce
Apples	Lima Beans
Apricots	Limes
Avocados	Millet
Bananas	Molasses
Beans	Mushrooms
Beets	Peaches
Blackberries	Pears
Broccoli	Peas
Brussels Sprouts	Pineapple
Buckwheat	Potatoes
Cabbage	Radishes
Cantalope	Raisins
Carrots	Raspberries
Cauliflower	Rutabagas
Celery	Sauerkraut
Cherries	Soybeans
Coconut	Spinach
Dates	Squash
Figs	Strawberries
Grapefruit	Tangerines
Grapes	Tomatoes
Green Beans	Watermelon
Lemons	

(LIMIT THE ACIDIC) ASH FOODS

This category should reflect 20% of your plate at meal time.

Flour
Refined Sugars
Dairy
Fish
Meat
Poultry
Peanut Butter
Nuts (most)
Plums
Prunes
Cranberries

(BETTER ACIDIC) ASH FOODS

Barley	Oatmeal
Blueberries	Pasta
Corn	Rice
Honey	
Legumes	*Neutral:*
	Butter

This is just an example of some of the foods associated with these categories. Not all foods are represented.

Making Meals a Priority

Eating the proper number of meals per day adds to your energy currency. Something we can all agree that we want more of. Food is energy, and like money, we either make deposits or withdrawals daily. This depends on the amount of live foods you partake in vs. processed. Studies suggest that it is important to consume 6 to 8 servings of vegetables and 3 to 5 servings of fruits per day. In addition, we must ensure that we are getting the right amount of protein, whole grains, healthy fats, vitamins, and nutrients. This can be achieved by eating 5 to 6 small nutrient dense meals per day. Therefore, skipping meals would not be the suggested route. This cookbook is broken down into sections—breakfast, mid-morning meals, soups, lunch, mid-afternoon meals, dinner, healthy sides, sweet treats, and drinks. There is also an eating schedule at the end to help you list the times you plan to eat each day.

What Is It Serving You?

Every action that we make will cause a reaction. For each recipe, you'll find the benefits for the body listed next to the LEAF symbol. Please note that I've only highlighted a few of the benefits, but many are bursting with much more.

Congratulations on your recent action to find new life giving recipes. Hope you enjoy the life you are about to be served and **L**et **E**very **A**ction **F**uel you.

Where do you start?

Before you can add the foods I'm about serve you, let's do a quick analysis of your cabinet/kitchen. Let's take inventory of the foods and items that you may currently have at your fingertips that are not the best options. The recipes in this book include clean ingredients and better alternatives to what you may be used to using. Below, you will find the top items that you want to beware of and their alternatives.

REFINED SUGARS

This is the first step and one of the top ingredients to look for. Time to go on a label hunt in your kitchen. Look for items that list ingredients such as sugar, high fructose corn syrup, dextrose, sucrose, fructose, maltose, and rice syrup. These are some of the refined sugars to pay close attention to. This may be alarming to you as you discover just how many items may list this ingredient. Sugar is hidden in more foods you purchase than you think. For example, you might find it in your nut butters, sauces, jelly, syrup, bread, instant oatmeal, hot chocolate, cereals, fruit snacks, cookies, beverages, and more. If you have a big pack of refined sugar, please get rid of it now. Refined sugars have been known to cause certain types of cancers, heart disease, diabetes, and the list continues. There are too many better sweeteners that will serve you more life than the others.

BETTER SUBSTITUTES

100 % organic pure maple syrup

- What is it serving you: Maple syrup is rich in antioxidants and a good source of magnesium, zinc, and calcium.

Organic raw honey

- What is it serving you: Raw honey has antibacterial and antifungal properties.

Dates

- What is it serving you: Dates are rich in B6, magnesium, and potassium.

SALT

The second step is to go through every item and look at the sodium content. According to the Journal of Environmental Health, our sodium to potassium ratio in our body is very important. There has been a huge change in this ratio over the years. In the past, potassium used to outnumber sodium by 10:1; now the ratio has dropped 1:3. Due to consuming more processed foods and eating out, many people are consuming three times more sodium than potassium on average. When this happens, there is a decrease in the alkalinity of the body and different diseases can increase like high blood pressure, water retention, headache, kidney disease, bone loss, and the list goes on. Some items high in sodium are canned soups, flavored boxed rice, spaghetti sauce, crackers, salad dressings, marinades, lunch meats, and more. If you have table salt in your cabinet, it's best to get rid of it.

BETTER SUBSTITUTES
Himalayan salt
What is it serving you: Himalayan salt is known for it's beautiful pink color because of the trace minerals. It contains more than 80 minerals and elements for the body. It also promotes healthy blood sugar, helps with the libido, helps lower blood sugar and helps with a healthy respiratory system.

OILS

The third step is to check for oils that contribute to trans fats. You want to be aware of items that have partially hydrogenated soybean oil, canola oil (also labeled rapeseed oil), or soybean oil. It's best to eliminate all hydrogenated oils as they can cause inflammation in the body. They are easy to use and cheap. It increases shelf life which is why many manufacturers use it. However, they don't increase your quality of life. Instead, trans fats raise your bad (LDL) cholesterol and lower your good (HDL) Cholesterol. They increase the risk of type 2 diabetes, stroke, and heart disease.

BETTER SUBSTITUTES
Olive Oil
What is it serving you: Olive oil helps your body maintain healthy cholesterol levels, helps with breast cancer risks, helps with the cardiovascular system, and helps to prevent stroke.

Unrefined organic coconut oil
What is it serving you: Coconut oil provides nourishment for the brain, it's rich in lauric acid which supports the body's immunity.

Avocado oil
What is it serving you: Avocado oil enhances the absorption of nutrients, reduces symptoms of arthritis, and is high in Lutein, an antioxidant that has benefits for the eyes.

Grape Seed oil
What is it serving you: Grapeseed oil is rich in vitamin E. Vitamin E is a vitamin that works as a fat-soluble antioxidant. It helps in protecting your cells from damaging free radicals that have been associated with cancer, heart disease, and other chronic illnesses.

Black Seed Oil
What is it serving you: Black seed oil has anti-fungal properties known to help with candida. It also has anti-cancer properties and has been said to lower blood pressure.

MAKE A GROCERY LIST

The fourth step is to make a grocery list. Now that you've removed items high in sugar, salt and partially hydrogenated soybean oil, it's time to revitalize your kitchen. This is a basic list of wonderful foods rich in macro- and micronutrients. Macronutrients are those we need more of like carbohydrates, proteins, and fats. Micronutrients are the important vitamins and minerals we need, such as vitamin D, vitamin B12 and iron. Please note that this is a basic list, so other foods that support healthy living may not be represented. The next time you're in the grocery store, check your cart and make sure it's full of foods that will provide you with optimal nutrition.

VEGETABLES

It's important to consume, at a minimum, 6 to 8 servings of vegetables per day.

- Artichokes
- Arugula
- Asparagus
- Broccoli/Broccolini
- Bok Choy
- Cabbage
- Carrots
- Cauliflower
- Celery
- Chard
- Collards
- Cucumber
- Dandelion Greens
- Eggplant
- Garlic
- Ginger
- Green Beans
- Jimaca
- Kale
- Leeks
- Salad (Mixed Greens)
- Mushrooms
- Onions
- Parsnips
- Peppers
- Radicchio
- Radishes
- Rutabaga
- Snow Peas
- Snap Peas
- Spaghetti Squash
- Spinach
- Tomato
- Turmeric Root
- Yellow Squash
- Yucca
- Zucchini

FRUIT

It's important to consume at least 3 to 5 servings of fruits per day.

- Apples
- Apricots
- Avocado
- Banana
- Blackberries
- Blueberries
- Cantaloupe
- Cherries
- Clementines
- Coconut
- Cranberries
- Dates
- Elderberries
- Figs
- Grapefruit
- Grapes
- Guava
- Honeydew Melon
- Jackfruit
- Kiwi
- Lemon
- Lime
- Mandarins
- Mango
- Mangosteen
- Mulberries
- Nectarines
- Olives
- Oranges
- Papaya
- Passion Fruit
- Peaches
- Pear
- Persimmon
- Pineapple
- Plantain
- Plums
- Pomegranate
- Prickly Pear
- Prunes
- Raspberries
- Strawberries
- Tangerine
- Watermelon

BEANS & GRAINS

Black Beans
Black-eyed Peas
Cannellini Beans
Lentils
Kidney Beans
Garbonzo Beans
Quinoa
Navy Beans
Oatmeal
Pigeon Peas
Millet
100% Cacao

NUTS

When choosing nuts, it's best to get raw nuts that are not roasted or salted.

Almonds
Brazil Nuts
Cashews
Hazelnuts
Macadamia Nuts
Peanuts
Pecans
Pistachios
Walnuts

SEEDS

Chia Seeds
Flax Seeds
Hemp seeds
Pine Nuts
Pomegranate Seeds
Poppy Seeds
Pumpkin Seeds
Sesame Seeds
Sunflower Seeds

FRESH HERBS

Mint
Basil
Thyme
Dill
Oregano
Rosemary
Tarragon

OILS

Olive Oil
Coconut Oil
Grapeseed Oil
Avocado Oil
Sesame Oil

ORGANIC VS. CONVENTIONAL

When choosing to buy organic vs. conventional, it's important to know the difference. Conventional farming does not use natural methods to promote growth but uses chemical and synthetics fertilizers. It also uses nitrates, growth hormones, and GMO's. Not only does this compromise the nutrient density of food, but it diminishes the nutrients in the soil. Organic farmers take a more natural approach with composting and a biodiversity method. This means natural manure, rotating their crops, and no added pesticides. This diminishes toxicity and dangerous substances that can affect the body. As a result, eating organic serves more nutrients and minerals.

WHAT ARE GMOS?

GMOs are Genetical Modified Organisms (or foods) whose genetic makeup has been modified in either a laboratory using genetic engineering or transgenic technology. This is not natural and many studies question the harmful affects it could have on the human body. It's best to look for the Non-GMO sign when shopping.

THE DIRTY DOZEN

It's important to buy organic whenever you can. However, for those that are budget conscious, I've often heard that buying organic is not always cost-effective. If there are times when you are picking and choosing what to buy organic vs. conventional, please refer to this list. It's known as the Dirty Dozen. This list was created that shows 12 crops that farmers use the most pesticides on. Out of all the vegetables, these were shown to have a residue of two or more pesticides. Most below are porous so be sure to purchase organic.

Strawberries	**Apples**	**Pears**
Spinach	**Grapes**	**Tomatoes**
Kale	**Peaches**	**Celery**
Nectarines	**Cherries**	**Potatoes**

THE CLEAN 15

These are the vegetables that show the lowest residue of pesticides.

Avocados	**Sweet peas (frozen)**	**Broccoli**
Sweet corn	**Eggplants**	**Mushrooms**
Pineapple	**Asparagus**	**Cabbage**
Onions	**Cauliflower**	**Honeydew melon**
Papaya	**Cantaloupes**	**Kiwi**

Give Thanks

ALWAYS GIVE THANKS BEFORE YOU PARTAKE.

Food is essential but it is not always intentional. This simply means that everyone may not always be consciously choosing what they are consuming. In addition to awakening your tastebuds, it's important to evaluate why you are eating and the emotion behind it. Eating out of fear, disappointment, pain, or even in a rush disrupts the digestive process. Your Eat-motions matter. So, before you eat, take a moment to center yourself with gratitude. Having a heart of thanksgiving for a healthy body to consume food and for your plate of food you are blessed to receive for the nourishment of your body.

Beginning with Power Breakfast

This meal is proven to be one of the most important meals of the day. This is primarily due to what happens before breakfast. For approximately 8 hours prior to this meal, your body has been fasting, resting, repairing, and digesting; therefore, it's time to restore your energy stores.

Breakfast is the time when you get a chance to consume a bit of the day before it begins. Awakening to the day with a grateful heart while fueling your body to recharge and restart. A time when you get to visualize your win and celebrate the day before you actually enter it. Let breakfast be that moment.

BaiSoul & Avocado Toast

Healthy food is good for the soul!

Toast has been a side for many during that big breakfast meal. It's usually topped with butter and smooth jam. This recipe is a way to give your toast a healthy balance and take it from a simple side to a full happy morning meal.

INGREDIENTS

1 large avocado

1/2 cup fresh basil

1 tsp olive oil

8 small red cherry tomatoes, halved

1/4 cup pumpkin seeds

Gluten free or fresh whole grain bread

Himalayan salt (optional)

PREPARATION

Lightly toast the bread.

Peel and cut the avocado. With a fork, mash the avocado. Spread the slightly mashed avocado across the bread or cut in chunks.

Evenly spread the tomatoes on top the avocado.

Sprinkle on the pumpkin seeds.

Add the fresh basil.

Drizzle on the olive oil.

Add a dash of himalayan salt on top for flavor.

WHAT IS IT SERVING YOU?

Avocados are one of the best healthy fats on the planet. They are also loaded with potassium and fiber.

Basil supports liver function, helps with digestion, and has vitamin K and calcium.

Tomatoes are high in lycopene which has been known to reduce the risk of heart disease and cancer. They are also high in vitamin C, K and potassium.

Pumpkin seeds contain healthy fats, protein, zinc and magnesium.

BREAKFAST 22

Heart-y Power Pancakes

Pancakes just make everybody smile! It's that sweet syrup drizzling down that mountain of a two or three stack of mouth-filled pleasure. Usually made with processed store bought mix, which has bleached white flour that is low in fiber. Pancakes typically are also low in protein which is essential at every meal. Therefore, pancakes are usually not the healthiest breakfast option. However, with this recipe, you can still enjoy pancakes and achieve a healthy meal high in fiber and protein. It's always better when they're homemade.

INGREDIENTS

1 large ripe banana

1 cup garbanzo bean flour

1 tsp cinnamon

1 tsp baking powder

2/3 cup almond milk

2 tsp extra virgin olive oil

PREPARATION

In a blender, put the banana and almond milk. Blend until smooth consistency.

Pour the smooth banana mixture into a medium size bowl.

Add the garbanzo bean flour, baking powder, and cinnamon. Mix well until smooth.

Heat your pan with oil on low to medium heat. Pour your batter into the pan according to the size you desire. You can tell the pancake is cooking well by the small bubbles evenly dispersed on top. Once you see those bubbles, flip to ensure it cooks fully throughout.

Top with fresh blueberries, strawberries, and drizzle with pure 100% maple syrup.

WHAT IS IT SERVING YOU?

Garbanzo bean flour is naturally gluten free. One cup provides the daily recommended amount of folate. It has twice as much as in wheat flour. It also has fewer calories than regular flour and is packed with more fiber and protein. It is also lower on the Glycemic index. This is the measure of how quick it takes food to break down into sugars that can spike your blood sugar.

Bananas are known for their high content of potassium. They are also high in vitamin B6. One medium banana provides a quarter of the daily requirement. The body cannot make this vitamin so it's important to obtain it from food.

The Bluberry French Kissed Toast

Let your lips taste something nutritious and delicious!

For those that are vegan and don't use egg, or for those watching their cholesterol and desire another alternative besides egg whites, flax meal is a great alternative for those recipes that call for eggs. French toast does not have to be that weekend calorie splurge, but a breakfast plate bursting with healthy benefits. For starters, Flaxseed (flax meal) has a combination of healthy omega-3 fatty acids, fiber, and antioxidants. It's also anti-inflammatory. It also prevents constipation, which will help the body better excrete after breakfast and for the remainder of the day. The chia will also help jumpstart your day. These seeds will balance your blood sugar levels and aid in healthy digestion. Like the flax, they also have omega-3's.

INGREDIENTS

Gluten free or whole grain bread

1 tsp chia seeds

1 T flax meal

1 cup almond milk

1 tsp pure vanilla

1 T coconut oil

PREPARATION

In a medium bowl whisk the almond milk, flax meal, chia seeds, pure vanilla, and cinnamon.

Heat your pan on medium with the coconut oil.

Lightly dip both sides of the bread into the batter without allowing the bread to fully submerge in the mixture.

Put the dipped bread into the heated pan turning each side after about 5 minutes or until lightly browned.

WHAT IS IT SERVING YOU?

Blueberries are known to be the king of antioxidants. They are also rich in iron, calcium, zinc, vitamin K, magnesium, manganese, help with aging and protect the body against

Chia seeds are high in fiber, omega-3 fatty acids, magnesium, phosphorus, manganese. They also contain B1, B2, B3, & zinc.

Flax seed meal is a great substitute for eggs. It contains lignans which are plant compounds that have antioxidant and estrogen properties, both of which can help lower the risk of cancer and improve health. Flax seeds have 800 times more lignans than other plant foods and are rich in Omega 3 fatty acids.

Arrowroot flour is a great thickening agent to substitute instead of cornstarch. Arrowroot also helps with digestion and helps the movement of the bowels. It's also gluten free.

THE TOPPING

What you put on top of this power breakfast matters. Many might choose a syrup, whip cream, or a sugary berry compote. This topping recipe has beauty for your French toast, your body, and your taste buds.

INGREDIENTS

1 cup fresh blueberries

1 tsp of arrowroot flour

1 T pure maple syrup

1 Bosc pear or pear of your choice

PREPARATION

In a medium heated pan, put in the blueberries, arrow root flour, and pure maple syrup.

Heat on medium low for about 8 to 10 minutes while stirring. Add a tsp of water to keep it from burning. Once thickened, remove from heat.

Melt vegan butter or oil of your choice in a medium saucepan. Add the the pear slices to the pan and flip after 2 minutes until each side is golden brown.

Top with blueberries, grilled pears and maple syrup.

The Royal Acai Bowl

You are regal and consuming breakfast in the morning is taking care of your castle for the remainder of the day. Your body is so important because it houses your purpose that you govern. Even it you are not super hungry in the morning, it's still important to give you body what it needs. Having a lighter and more refreshing breakfast is the way to go on those not so hungry days.

INGREDIENTS

1 pack pure açaí sugar free purée, frozen

1/2 cup blueberries, frozen

Handful spinach

1/2 banana, frozen

2 tsp chia seeds

1/2 cup frozen strawberries

1/4 cup almond milk

PREPARATION

Blend on high. The consistency should be thicker than that of a smoothie. Pour into a bowl to serve.

Topping - fresh sliced bananas and raw shredded coconut. Can also top with homemade granola (recipe on page 158).

Please note: açaí packs may be purchased at Trader Joe's or Whole Foods.

WHAT IS IT SERVING YOU?

Acai berries are a super fruit loaded with antioxidants which prevent cancer.

Blueberries are high in antioxidants.

Bananas contain potassium.

Strawberries contain 51.5% of your daily requirement of vitamin C per serving. One serving also has 21 mg of folate per serving which is an vitamin for pregnant woman. It helps to develop the baby's brain, spinal cord, and skull.

Chia seeds contain about 5.6 grams of protein per ounce. They are also high in omega-3 fatty acids, fiber, iron, and calcium.

BREAKFAST 28

Oatmeal Apple Sunrise

Oatmeal has the ability to turn from a boring bowl of whole grains to a bursting bowl of sweet flavors. I'm not speaking of the instant variety packs that require just a little hot water. Many of those contain refined sugars and artificial flavors that will deplete your energy reserve later in the day. Take a little time to store the optimal energy you deserve. So, instead of choosing the baked apple flavored packets, use real apples to take your oatmeal to the next nutritional level.

INGREDIENTS

1 1/2 cups oatmeal

2 apples

1 tsp coconut oil

1 tsp cinnamon

1 tsp nutmeg

1 T raisins

1/3 cup almond milk

2 cups water

3 tsp honey

PREPARATION

Preheat the oven to 350 degrees.

Core & dice apples. (I like to leave the skin on for this dish. Plus the skin will provide you extra nutrients.)

In a small bowl, mix coconut oil, cinnamon, nutmeg, and maple syrup. Stir well. Add the apples. Mix until sauce coats the apples. In a pan, bake for 20 minutes.

When the apples have 7 to 8 minutes remaining, mix water and almond milk together and bring to a boil to form the oatmeal. Add raisins to apple mixture in oven.

Add the oats to the boiling water/almond milk, lower to medium/low and stir until liquid is absorbed.

Place oatmeal in bowl, top with apple mixture, and top with walnuts for protein.

WHAT IS IT SERVING YOU?

Oats contain a powerful soluble fiber called beta-glucan. It also lowers cholesterol levels, and have a group of antioxidants called avenanthramides that are only found in oats.

Apples are rich in fiber, vitamin C, vitamin K, & Quercetin. They also contain polyphenols which have antioxidant effects and lowers cholesterol. Many of these polyphenols are concentrated in the peel.

Breakfast Quinoa Wow Bowl

INGREDIENTS

1 cup quinoa

2 cups water

1 apple

2 T walnuts

1 tsp cinnamon

2/3 cup almond milk

Maple syrup - sweeten to taste

PREPARATION

Rinse a cup of Quinoa and add 2 cups water in a pot.

Bring to a boil and turn down to medium.

Simmer on the stove for about 12 to 15 minutes until tender. Turn off stove.

Dice apples. If you prefer your apples a little tender, add them to the pot of quinoa immediately upon turning the stove off. Cover and let sit for 5 minutes. If you prefer them crunchy like the picture, drain the water from the quinoa, and put the quinoa in a medium bowl. Add the apples, walnuts, almond milk, cinnamon, and maple syrup. Stir and enjoy!

Serve warm.

WHAT IS IT SERVING YOU?

Quinoa is high in fiber (known to be one of the highest fiber grains), protein, quercetin, and contains all 9 of the essential amino acids.

Walnuts have the highest Omega-3 amount than any other nut, also rich in antioxidants.

Apples contain soluable fiber which help to lower blood pressure and bowel regularity. In addition, many antioxidants and nutrients are found in the apple peel

Millet & the Eggless Omelet

Eggs are a breakfast tradition and staple for many. They are full of protein, but they are also acidic. Early in this book, you learned about the importance of ensuring an alkaline and acidic balance during your meals. I'm not suggesting that eggs be removed from the diet, but I do suggest adding more life to your breakfast. Next time you think of just having eggs and grits consider a side of vegetables to accompany those eggs and replace the grits with a healthier grain like millet.

INGREDIENTS

1 large tomato

1 red/orange/yellow bell pepper

1 cup spinach

1/2 red onion

1/2 cup mushrooms

1 jalapeño

2 tsp olive oil

Himalayan salt to taste

1 cup raw millet

2 cups water

1/2 diced onion

PREPARATION

Dice the veggies and sauté in olive oil. Season with himalayan salt.

In a large, dry saucepan, toast the raw millet over medium heat for 4-5 minutes or until it turns a rich golden brown.

Sauté diced onion and olive oil in a separate pan. Pour the onions in with the millet.

Add the water and himalayan salt to the millet and stir.

Increase the heat to high and bring the mixture to a boil. Lower the heat to a simmer and cover the pot.

Simmer until the grains absorb most of the water (they'll continue soaking it up as they sit), about 15 minutes.

Millet is best served warm.

WHAT IS IT SERVING YOU?

Millet is rich in both insoluble and soluble fiber. It is also protein-rich and high in vitamin A.
Bell peppers are high in vitamin C and rich in antioxidants.
Tomatoes contain lycopene which is linked to reducing the risk of heart disease.
Spinach is high in calcium, potassium and a good source of iron.
Red onion contains the antioxidant, quercetin, which helps boost the immune system.
Mushrooms contain vitamin D.
Jalapeño contains vitamin B6, vitamin C, and they are known to help with pain relief.

Small, energizing mid-morning meals

You have now been launched into your day and you're thriving with productivity. It's time to take a small break to feed the body a quick, nutrient dense, small meal. This meal should consist of raw protein and a live food. Many people may consider this time "snack time" and be tempted to grab a granola bar or string cheese and pretzels. Those are examples of processed items and not a small meal that will provide you optimal energy. You want to ensure that this meal has vitamins and life to continue to support your daily thrive.

A small energized meal is a shot of power to fuel your next 2 to 3 hours. A small side of life paired with a raw protein. It may be a small plate but cheers to the amount of energy it will create.

When adding nuts to your small energizing meals, it's important to ensure that they are raw, not roasted or salted. Also, they should be paired with a live food that is not processed. Below are three great examples. However, in this section, we will explore a few recipes that will take your small mid-morning meal to a whole new level of flavor.

Oranges & Almonds

WHAT IS IT SERVING YOU?

Oranges are high in vitamin C, prevent skin damage, & help control blood sugar levels .

Almonds* contain protein, fiber, vitamin E.

Blueberries & Walnuts

WHAT IS IT SERVING YOU?

Blueberries are rich in antioxidants.

Walnuts are high in Omega 3's & protein.

Apples & Brazil Nuts

WHAT IS IT SERVING YOU?

Apples contain quercetin & fiber.

Brazil Nuts are high in selenium.

MID-MORNING MEALS 38

Carrot & ParSlay Salad

Slay those free redicals

INGREDIENTS

2 cups shredded organic carrots

2-3 T finely chopped parsley

1/2 cup walnuts

1/3 cup golden raisins

1/2 fresh squeezed lemon

1 T olive oil

1 clove ginger

2 tsp honey

PREPARATION

Pour shredded carrots into a medium bowl.

Blend the olive oil, ginger, honey and lemon.

Add the parsley, walnuts, and raisins to the bowl with the carrots.

Add the sauce from the blender and mix it all together.

Season with himalayan salt to taste.

Cover and refrigerate until ready to serve.

WHAT IS IT SERVING YOU?

Carrots contain beta carotene, fiber, vitamin K1, potassium.

Parsley is high in vitamin A, C, & K.

Walnuts contain omega-3 fatty acids which supports brain function as we age.

Ginger contains gingerol which is a bioactive compound in ginger. It is known for it's medicinal properties that help with inflammation and removing free radicals from the body.

Golden raisins are a great source of fiber, iron, and calcium.

The Golden Sunflower

The dressing on top of of this salad adds to the value of it, making it golden like the beets. When choosing a dressing, it's important to know what it is serving you. Many are filled with unwanted oils, sugars, preservatives, and sodium. A great dressing alternative is an aged balsamic. A good one should be thick with a rich flavor, certified from Modena, Italy, and free from additives.

INGREDIENTS

2 small golden beets

2 small Chioggia beets

1/4 cup sunflower seeds

2 cups arugula

1 T aged balsamic

PREPARATION

Place arugula on your plate.

Cut the beets in triangles and spread evenly across arugula.

Top with sunflower seeds.

Drizzle with an aged balsamic.

WHAT IS IT SERVING YOU?

Golden beets are packed with Vitamin C, manganese, and folate.

Sunflower seeds contain vitamin E, selenium, and zinc.

Arugula contains folate, vitamin c, and potassium.

Quality aged balsamic contains natural probiotics that aid in healthy digestion. It's also a good source of calcium, potassium, and magnesium.

The Melon & Jicama Medley

INGREDIENTS

1 medium jicama

1 cup fresh pineapple

1 cup watermelon

1 cup cucumber

1 T olive oil

1 fresh lime

1/2 cups walnuts

PREPARATION

Cut the jicama, pineapple, watermelon, and cucumber into cubes. Place into a medium bowl.

Toss in the olive oil.

Squeeze with fresh lime.

Add a dash of himalayan salt (optional).

Top with walnuts and enjoy!

WHAT IS IT SERVING YOU

Jicama is a hydrating vegetable that is made up of close to 90% water. Many will explain the taste as a cross between an apple and a potato. It is a great source of prebiotic fibers which help with the digestive system. It also contains many essential vitamins and minerals, including vitamin C, folate, potassium, and magnesium.

Pineapple is rich in manganese which supports bone health. It also has bromelain which reduces oxidative stress and inflammation in the joints.

Watermelon is 92% water which helps with hydration. It is rich in antioxidants lycopene and vitamin C.

Cucumber is 96% water and fiber which is a combination that can aid in bowl regularity and is high in vitamin K.

The citric acid in **lime** is known to help with weight loss. Limes also contain magnesium and vitamin C.

Walnuts contain omega 3 and omega 6 fatty acids which support brain health. They also contain selenium and iodine also known to help with healthy brain function.

45 SERVING YOU LIFE

The Beauty & the Beet Salad

INGREDIENTS

2 ripe pears

3 medium beets

3 cups arugula

3 T raw pistachios

2 T balsamic vinegar

1 T olive oil

1/2 tsp honey

1/2 small lemon

PREPARATION

Cut pears into square cubes keeping the skin on.

Grate beets into shreds with a grater.

Put arugula in a medium bowl.

Mix in the pears & beets.

Toss in the pistachios.

Top with the dressing listed below.

THE DRESSING

Whisk together **1 tablespoon balsamic vinegar, 1 tablespoon pure virgin olive oil, 1/2 teaspoon honey** and **2 squeezes of lemon.**

🌿 WHAT IS IT SERVING YOU?

Beets commonly referred to as "crimson spinach" have nutrient dense similarities like that of one of the most nutrient dense greens — spinach. Both are rich in folate, iron, and betaine. Beets also lower blood pressure while fighting inflammation in the body.

Arugula is rich in calcium and folate. The copper in arugula stimulates the growth of white blood cells.

Pears are high in fiber and potassium.

Pistachios contain antioxidants which support eye health and help maintain long-term vision. They are also an excellent source of vitamin B6.

Get cozy with Soup

Soup is usually that go to bowl of warmth when the body is not feeling the greatest. Most will grab a can of soup from the nearest grocery store or stop at the nearest restaurant. The hope is to provide some comfort to the body, take a break from a large meal, or help the body heal. The problem is that most soup in cans and from restaurants are usually very high in sodium. That's contrary to what the body needs to aid in recovery. Show your body some love and make it yourself. Your body will respond with love.

The Butternut Bae Soup

INGREDIENTS

1 medium to large butternut squash

1 apple

1 cup coconut milk

1 cup low sodium vegetable stock

2 cloves garlic

3 stalks celery

1 T olive oil

1 tsp cinnamon

1 tsp nutmeg

Himalayan salt to taste

PREPARATION

Cut butternut squash and apples into squares and toss in a light coconut oil.

Preheat oven to 400 degrees.

Arrange the coated butternut cubes on a parchment-lined long baking sheet and place them in the oven to roast for 25 to 30 minutes.

Half way through baking, put the apples in the oven with the butternut squash and cook for an additional 15 minutes.

Remove and let cool.

In a medium saucepan, add 1 T olive oil and sauté celery, garlic, and onions.

In a blender, combine vegetable stock, sautéed celery, onions, and garlic, and blend on high, then add butternut squash, apples and the second cup of veggie broth. Next, add coconut milk and blend on high until smooth.

Place blended smooth mixture into a medium or large sauce pan. Heat and serve.

Top with a little cayenne pepper, pumpkin seeds, and enjoy!

WHAT IS IT SERVING YOU?

Butternut squash is an immune booster loaded with vitamin A, C, magnesium, and potassium.

Apples contain antioxidants that have been shown to slow the growth of cancer cells.

Garlic is rich in vitamin B6, manganese, and vitamin C.

Celery contains vitamin A, vitamin K, and folate.

Lentil Love Soup

INGREDIENTS

2 cups lentils

1 medium onion

4 cups low sodium veggie broth

1 clove garlic

2 stalks celery

2 T olive oil

2 cups water

4 fresh roma tomatoes

1 long green onion

2 long organic carrots

Himalayan salt to taste

PREPARATION

Finely dice onions, garlic, celery and green onion.

Cut carrots into thin circles, then cut the tomatoes into cubes.

In a large saucepan, heat the olive oil on medium and add the diced vegetables. Sauté until tender.

Rinse lentils and add water and lentils to the pot.

Bring to a soft boil, cover with a lid, and let it simmer on low.

Lower heat to medium and add the the cut tomatoes and carrots.

Continue to cook for 25 minutes until lentils are tender and everything cooks together.

Himalayan salt to taste.

WHAT IS IT SERVING YOU?

Having all the ingredients simmer together provides a host of nutrients for the body. The **lentils** provide a complete protein, the **celery** aids in digestion, the **onions** are antibacterial which helps with infection, the **tomatoes** carry antioxidants, and the **carrots** add beta-carotene which contributes to healthy mucus membranes.

Sweet Beans of Harmony Soup

INGREDIENTS

1 cup navy beans

1 cup kidney beans

1 cup black beans

1 cup pinto beans

4 medium fresh tomatoes

3 cloves garlic, minced

2 stalks celery, chopped

1 onion

2 tsp ground cumin

1 T smoked paprika

2 tsp fresh lime juice

1/2 cup fresh kale

2 cups low sodium vegetable stock

1 bay leaf

Himalayan salt to taste

PREPARATION

Cooking dried beans is easy! Here's what you need to do:

Rinse beans thoroughly. I recommend that you soak your beans before you cook them. It helps them digest better, making them less gaseous as well as helping them cook faster. To soak, place the dried beans in a large bowl and add enough helping the water to cover by 2 to 3 inches. Discard any beans that float. Cover and allow the beans to soak for at least 8 hours, or overnight. In the morning, drain and rinse the soaked beans, and they are ready to cook!

Transfer the soaked beans to a large pot and cover them with 2 inches of water. If you prefer not to soak your beans, rinse them in a fine mesh strainer before you add them to the pot. Bring the water to a boil, reduce the heat, and simmer for 30 minutes.

Add seasonings & continue cooking. Cook according to package instructions if in a hurry, but I recommend soaking them overnight to make them easier to digest. Cook until the beans are tender, adding more water if they begin to look dry or do not taste soft. Depending upon the amount of beans you are making and the freshness of the beans, the cooking time can vary. Check them every 30 minutes for tenderness and make sure there is at least 1 1/2 inches of water covering the beans. (If you are pressed for time and you are using can beans, be sure they are organic and free of salt. Also ensure that the cans have a BPA free lining.)

In a medium saucepan, heat the olive oil on medium. Add the onion, garlic, celery, bay leaf, and spices. Saute for about 5 minutes. Stir in the tomatoes, cooked beans, and veggie broth. Bring to a slow simmer for another 15 minutes. Add the cumin and paprika. Season with himalayan salt to taste. Then, add the kale. Cook for an additional two minutes to give the kale a chance to soften. It's now ready to serve!

WHAT IS IT SERVING YOU?

Beans and legumes are important to add to meals throughout the week. They contain amino acids, which are protein blocks that the body employs to heal and to make new tissues, such as muscle, hair, blood, skin, and bone. They also contain folate which helps to make healthy red blood cells.

Give your day an energy punch!
Lunch

This is that much awaited time for many all across the nation, a break to recharge and refuel. Whether you are working or not, lunch is necessary for increasing metabolism and ensuring the body is provided the necessary vitamins and nutrients. There is still a whole lot of day ahead and the meal decisions we make during this time will play a major role in our productivity and energy for the remainder of the day. Choose wisely with vibrant colors to achieve optimal fueling meals.

The Power Fuel Salad

Having a great salad is a phenomenal way to ensure that you are receiving all of your necessary vitamins at a particular meal. Achieving this is an art, just like your salad can be.

BUILDING A POWERHOUSE SALAD

First step - Your foundation is important and it needs to be a strong one. The first layer of strength are those power greens. All are not created equal as far as the level of nutrients they provide. For example, iceberg lettuce and romaine have been chosen as the first and only foundational option for many salads. Though filled with water and low in fat and calories, they are not as nutrient dense as some of the others. Those powerhouse greens full of vitamins and better options would include; kale, spinach, water cress, arugula, dandelion greens, Swiss chard, collard greens, mustard greens, and red and purple cabbage.

Second step - Choose at least three vegetables that have a variety of colors. Choosing the different colors not only ensures that you will receive an array of vitamins and nutrients but specific colors support different organs in the body. Take red vegetables for example, they support heart health.

Third step - Choose a healthy protein. It's important to include protein at every meal. Great options include legumes, raw nuts, and seeds.

Fourth step - Choose a healthy grain. An example might be quinoa or brown rice.

Fifth step - Add a healthy fat or some omegas. This could include an avocado.

Sixth step - Avoid dressings that are high in oils and contain trans fats, sugars, are high in sodium, and include a long list of ingredients. It's better to make your own dressing. Try mixing olive oil with an aged balsamic vinaigrette. It's naturally delicious and will give you both a healthy fat (olive oil) and probiotics (the aged balsamic vinaigrette).

Finally, enjoy your power salad!

LUNCH 58

Grilled Eggplant & Veggie Linguini

INGREDIENTS

2 medium eggplants

1 red onion

1 green bell pepper

1 yellow bell pepper

1 red bell pepper

1 tsp fresh oregano

1 tsp dried oregano

1 box lentil pasta

4 cups water

2 garlic cloves, pureed

Himalayan salt to taste

2 T olive oil

PREPARATION

Wash eggplant and cut into quarter-like circles. Cut onion and bell peppers in french fry pieces.

Combine olive oil, pureed garlic, fresh cut oregano and salt with veggies in a large zip lock bag.

If using a grill: place eggplant approximately 1/2 inch apart and cook on each side for about 3 minutes before turning.

If cooking in the oven: place the eggplant and veggies on parchment paper. Preheat the oven to 425 degrees and roast for about 13 to 15 minutes.

While the veggies are cooking, add water to a large saucepan, and bring the water to a vigorous boil.

Add the pasta and cook for about 10 minutes until the noodles are soft. Remove from heat and drain the water. Add a 1/2 tsp of olive oil to the noodles so they do not stick together, and place cooked pasta on a plate.

Top with the grilled vegetables. Sprinkle with a little dried oregano and enjoy.

WHAT IS IT SERVING YOU?

Lentil Pasta contains 15 to 25 grams of protein per serving.

Eggplant is high in vitamin C, K, B6, fiber, and potassium to name a few. It has phytonutrients which is a natural chemical said to help with brain function and mental health. It is also known to help with anemia.

Red bell pepper is considered the most nutritious of all the other bell peppers because it's been on the vine the longest. It has 253% of the needed daily vitamin C and 73% of the daily need of vitamin A.

The Black Bean & Avocado Fit-Fusion

INGREDIENTS

3 cups cooked black beans (If using a can, be sure it's BPA free and the beans are organic with no added salt)

1 red onion, chopped

4 roma tomatoes, chopped

3 oz. fresh, roughly chopped cilantro

2 avocados, peeled & chopped

1 mango, peeled & chopped

1 red, 1 yellow & 1 orange bell pepper

2 fresh limes

Himalayan salt to taste

1/4 cup olive oil

PREPARATION

If cooking dried beans: Soak the beans in cold water overnight. Rinse and drain. Place the beans into a large heavy-based pan, cover with water and bring to a boil. Reduce the heat and simmer for 1 ½ hours, or until tender. Drain and cool slightly.

If using beans from the can: Rinse thoroughly.

Place the beans, onion, tomatoes, pepper, cilantro, avocado and mango into a large bowl. Squeeze in the fresh lime juice. Drizzle with olive oil. Season with salt to taste, and toss to combine.

Serving suggestion: Use this mixture to top cilantro brown rice.

WHAT IS IT SERVING YOU?

Avocado is high in potassium & fiber.
Black Beans are high in fiber, protein, B6, potassium and folate.
Red onion contains fructooligosaccharides which are substances that act as prebiotics.
Tomatoes are high in the vitamin biotin which is known to promote hair growth.
Cilantro contains chlorophyll. This green pigment helps to detoxify the body from the inside out.
Lime rejuvenates skin and strengthens collagen due to it's high amount of vitamin C.
Bell peppers contain fiber, iron, folate, vitamin C, and potassium.

Cauliflower Tacos

Causing your energy to bloom!

INGREDIENTS

1 large head of cauliflower, cored and broken into florets

4 cloves garlic, minced

2 tbs olive oil

1/2 cup canned tomato sauce (no salt with BPA free lining for the can)

4 tsp chili powder

1 tsp liquid smoke

1 large onion

1 tsp smoked paprika

1/2 cup cilantro

1 tsp himalayan salt

2 cups cooked black beans (optional)

PREPARATION

In a medium sauce pan, add 2 tbs olive oil. Add the minced garlic and onions. Sauté for 2 to 3 minutes.

Add the tomato paste, chili powder, smoked paprika, cilantro and salt. If a little thick, add 1/2 tsp more olive oil.

Place the cauliflower florets in a large bowl. Add the liquid tomato sauce mixture that was made in the saucepan. Stir until every floret is covered.

Preheat oven to 400 degrees.

Place cauliflower with coated mixture on a baking sheet. Cook for 20 to 25 minutes until golden brown.

Place the cauliflower on your shell first. Then, add tomatoes, cilantro, or shredded spinach/lettuce. Top with the fresh sauce and enjoy.

*Add black beans for protein.

WHAT IS IT SERVING YOU?

Cauliflower contains choline which many foods do not have. Choline helps with the nervous system and brain development. It also contains sulforaphane which is an antioxidant that studies show being helpful in suppressing cancer development.

VEGAN LIME DRESSING

Combine **1/2 cup coconut milk**, **1/2 cup cashews**, **1/4 tsp himalayan salt**, **3 ounces lime juice**, **1/2 avocado**, **2 T coconut milk plain yogurt** and **1/4 cup cilantro** in a blender or food processor and blend until smooth.

Jammin' Jackfruit Tacos

Make your body move!

INGREDIENTS

Jackfruit

4 cloves garlic, minced

2 tbs olive oil

1/2 cup canned tomato sauce
(no salt with BPA free lining for the can)

4 tsp chili powder

1 large onion

2 tsp cumin

1 tsp coriander

1 tsp liquid smoke

1 1/2 tsp himalayan salt

PREPARATION

In a medium sauce pan, add 2 tbs olive oil. Add the minced garlic and onions. Sauté for 2 to 3 minutes.

Add the tomato paste, liquid smoke, chili powder, cumin, coriander and salt. If a little thick, add 1/2 tsp more olive oil.

Place the jackfruit in a large bowl. Add the liquid tomato sauce mixture from the saucepan. Stir until every floret is covered.

Preheat oven to 400 degrees.

Place cauliflower with coated mixture on a baking sheet. Cook for 20 to 25 minutes until golden brown.

Place the cauliflower on your shell. Then, add tomatoes, cilantro, or shredded spinach/lettuce.

*Add black beans for protein.

WHAT IS IT SERVING YOU?

Jackfruit is an excellent source of phytonutrients like lignans, isoflavones, and saponins, all of which are said to have anti-aging properties. Jackfruit is also loaded with fiber and has about 3 grams of protein per cup.

Broc & Bok Joy

INGREDIENTS

1 pound bok choy

2 cups broccoli

1 cup sliced portobello mushrooms

2 inch chunk ginger

1 small sweet onion

2 T olive oil

1 tsp sesame seeds

2 T honey

2 T sesame oil

PREPARATION

Turn the bok choy lengthwise, and then cut into smaller pieces. Separate the stalks from the leaves.

Chop the onion. Chop the ginger into 3 smaller chunks. Cut the mushrooms.

Heat oil in a large saucepan an sauté garlic and onions for 3 minutes. Add the mushrooms and saute for an additional 3 minutes. Remove from heat.

In a high power blender, blend ginger, soy sauce alternative (Braggs amino), honey, sesame oil.

Return pan to medium heat and add blended sauce to pan. Stir until the vegetables are covered in the sauce for 3 to 5 minutes.

Season with himalayan salt, sprinkle sesame seeds evenly.

Enjoy with brown rice and a salad!

WHAT IS IT SERVING YOU?

Broccoli contains calcium, vitamin K, and zinc.

Bok Choy is high in beta carotene, vitamin C and vitamin E.

Portobello mushroom contains selenium, copper and potassium.

Confetti Quinoa

Quinoa is an amazing grain that will take on different flavors. It's known as one of the world's healthiest grains.

INGREDIENTS

1 cup quinoa

2 cups water

3 small roma tomatoes

1 medium cucumber

1 cup of chopped spinach

1 fresh lime

2 tsp olive oil

1 tsp Himalayan salt

PREPARATION

In a medium pot bring quinoa and water to a boil.

Turn down and simmer for 8 minutes then, turn off and cover. Allow the quinoa to cook.

Cut the tomatoes, cucumber, spinach and cilantro into small pieces and put all of the ingredients in a medium serving bowl.

Add the quinoa to the bowl of vegetables and mix well. Squeeze in the fresh lime and olive oil. Mix again until the lime and olive oil is coated throughout.

Season with Himalayan salt to taste.

Let it chill and serve.

WHAT IS IT SERVING YOU?

Quinoa is a super grain loaded with protein, magnesium, folate, & quercetin. The source of protein stems from a rare amino acid called Lysine that happens to be in Quinoa, but not many other grains. It's also rich in vitamin B2 known to help with headaches by its ability to expand the blood vessels in the brain.

Tomatoes contain a flavonoid in the skin called naringenin that helps with inflammation.

Cucumbers are full of potassium, vitamin A, and vitamin K.

Spinach is high in iron which helps with anemia and a good source of calcium which helps with bone health.

Sweet Veggie Brown

There are different colors of quinoa and I like to use them for different recipes. Brown quinoa has a slight sweeter taste than white and is a bit heartier.

INGREDIENTS

2 cups water

1/2 red onion

1/2 fresh lemon

1/2 fresh lime

1/2 sweet onion

1 cup black beans

1 T coconut sugar

1 T olive oil

1/2 tsp himalayan salt

1 can cooked black beans
(be sure it is organic, salt free,
and the can has BPA free liner).
Or use dried beans and cook them.

1 T apple cider vinegar

1/2 cup cilantro

Himalayan salt to taste

PREPARATION

Bring 2 cups water to boil along with oil and salt. Rinse quinoa in a mesh strainer with cold water, and add to boiling water. Reduce heat and simmer for 12 to 15 minutes. Remove from heat, cover, and allow liquid to completely absorb.

Open can of black beans, and rinse well.

Dice all the veggies, and place in medium bowl.

Mix apple cider vinegar, coconut sugar, lime, lemon, and salt in a small bowl.

Add liquid mixture to bowl of mixed vegetables and mix well.

Add black beans and mix again.

Place the quinoa in a bowl and top with the vegetable mixture.

WHAT IS IT SERVING YOU?

Quinoa has naturally occurring plant chemicals that are said to offer great benefits to our health. It has a higher nutrient density than rice and is known for it's source of protein and fiber.

> "WELLNESS IS LOVE WITH INTENTION. IT IS A BEAUTIFUL GIFT THAT WE GIVE OURSELVES AND IT NEVER STOPS YIELDING REWARDS. JUST LIKE WITH THAT SPECIAL SOMEONE, WELLNESS DESERVES OUR PASSIONATE ATTENTION."

Small, energizing mid-afternoon meals

Having a small mid-afternoon meal is taking time to pause with gratefulness for the productivity you've already given throughout your day. Understanding that a bit of added fuel will push you even further. That simple small meal of a raw protein and a live food, particularly some vegetables, will give you just the boost you need. We need to ensure we consume 6 to 8 servings of vegetables per day and adding small meals is a great way to achieve this. It's also important to include protein at every meal so these small suggestions are great combinations. They contribute to your 5 to 6 meals a day which helps boost your metabolism.

Relish in the Radish

My desire is to awaken your taste buds to vegetables you probably have not consumed in a while. There are a plethora of them waiting for you to explore.

Take the radish. There are so many different types of these nutrient dense root vegetables. The most common one is the Cherry Belle which is the red flavorful ball many thinly slice or toss whole in their salad.

A beautiful type of radish you may not eat as often as the Cherry Belle is the Watermelon radish. The beauty lies within this root vegetable and is shown once it is cut. It will bring beauty to any plate.

INGREDIENTS

2 thinly sliced Watermelon radishes

2 Figs

1/2 cup of walnuts

2 cups fresh dandelion greens

Sweet balsamic dressing

PREPARATION

Slice watermelon radish into thin slices and then cut each slice into four smaller slices.

Chop dandelion greens to individual leaves.

Cut figs into small pieces.

Chop walnuts.

Combine all ingredients in a bowl.

Drizzle with a quality sweet balsamic dressing.

WHAT IS IT SERVING YOU?

Radishes are high in vitamin A, C, K, B6, E, calcium, magnesium, iron, zinc, fiber, and are rich in antioxidants. They are also known to help with digestion and skin.

Dandelion greens contain high levels of the antioxidant beta-carotene. They also help to keep the liver healthy and reduce inflammation in the body and so much more.

Walnuts help to keep your heart healthy. They are a natural plant-based source of Omega 3's.

Figs are high in fiber. Studies have also shown that they help to reduce the production of glucose in the liver which can help with diabetes. They also are a natural aphrodisiac known to help with erectile dysfunction.

MID-AFTERNOON MEALS 78

The Scrumptious Cabbage Crunch

INGREDIENTS

1 medium head of cabbage

1 cup almonds

1 T sesame seeds

1 T honey

1 T toasted sesame oil

Apple cider vinegar

1/2 tsp Himalayan salt

PREPARATION

Cut cabbage into long shredded slices. Combine shredded cabbage, almonds, and sesame seeds in a bowl.

Whisk together honey, sesame oil, apple cider vinegar, and Himalayan salt. Pour over salad and stir to combine.

WHAT IS IT SERVING YOU?

Cabbage is high in vitamin K, vitamin C and folate.

Almonds contain vitamin E, magnesium, fiber and protein

Sesame seeds are full of bone building minerals such as calcium. magnesium, manganese and copper.

Apple cider vinegar lowers blood sugar levels and contains amino acids, iron, and magnesium.

Hummus Stuffed Cucumber

Hummus is a great side protein that pairs well with many veggies to complete a great energizing snack. However, many will buy the store bought round container filled with preservatives and added salt not recognizing how easy it is to make. Here's a simple recipe to stuff your body with what matters while you leave out what doesn't.

INGREDIENTS

Chickpeas/garbanzo beans - if in the can, ensure that it says organic, no salt added, and BPA free

1/4 cup tahini

1/2 cup water

1 clove garlic

4 T extra virgin olive oil

1 fresh lemon

Himalayan salt

2 cucumbers

1 cup micro greens

PREPARATION

If from the can: Rinse the chickpeas and drain until they are dry.

If using dry beans: Place them in a large bowl and cover with water. Soak 8 hours or over night. After soaking, drain and put the beans in a large pot. Fill with water until the water is approximately 2 inches above the beans. Bring to a rapid boil and lower the heat and allow the beans to simmer and cook for about an hour. Once cooked, drain the water and let the beans cool.

Once drained from the can, or cooled if you are cooking them, place chickpeas in a blender. Add the fresh lemon juices (pre-squeezed to ensure no seeds), olive oil, tahini, and salt. Blend on high until smooth.

Cut the cucumbers in half. Gently remove the inside of the cucumber. This is where you can have fun. Feel free to carve them as you'd like. Just be sure to have an opening for the hummus.

Top with micro greens and you've got yourself a delicious small energizing meal.

WHAT IS IT SERVING YOU?

Tahini is made out of ground sesame seeds. It has just as much protein as most nuts and milk, and is high in Thiamin (vitamin B1) & vitamin B6. Both of these are important for energy production which further makes this a small energizing meal.

Chickpeas are known to promote bone health. They are rich in iron and calcium. They are also full of selenium, magnesium, iron, fiber, potassium, and B vitamins.

Smokin' Red Pepper Hummus

Fire up your energy!

INGREDIENTS

2 cups garbanzo beans

1 red pepper

1 clove garlic

1/4 cup olive oil

1 tsp liquid smoke

3 T tahini

1 T water

1 tsp smoked paprika

Himalayan salt to taste

PREPARATION

Heat oven to a high broil.

Put whole bell pepper in oven three inches from broiler. Roast each side for 5 minutes. The sides will turn black as they roast. Remove from oven and cover bell pepper in a dish with a lid for 15 minutes. This will trap heat and moisture to make it easier to peel the skin. Remove bell pepper, take out the core, peel the skin and discard it.

In a blender, add the bell pepper, tahini, garlic, water, smoked paprika, liquid smoke, himalayan salt, and lemon juice.
Blend on high until smooth.

Add the olive oil and blend again for 2 minutes or until smooth.

Serve with your favorite vegetables.

WHAT IS IT SERVING YOU?

Many people have never purchased **tahini**. It's made out of ground sesame seeds. It has just as much protein as most nuts and milk. It's also high in Thiamin (vitamin B1) & vitamin B6. Both of these are important for energy production which will make this a small energizing meal.

Chickpeas are known to promote bone health. They are rich in iron and calcium. Not only will that help to prevent osteoporosis but there are other benefits to support heart health. It's full of selenium, magnesium, iron, fiber, potassium, and B vitamins.

Red bell peppers are known to be the healthiest of all the other color peppers, because they have been on the vine the longest. The have 11 times more beta-carotene and 1.5 times more vitamin C than the others.

Ending the day like a winner!
Dinner

Dinner is the time to sit back and enjoy a balanced meal while basking in the greatness of the vivacious day you just had. It's also the time to make up for the vegetables, fruits, grains and other nutrients you probably missed throughout the day. For example, you are supposed to have 6 to 8 servings of vegetables per day. If you did not achieve that with your previous meals, dinner is the time to ensure you make up your nutrition deficit and cross your daily nutritious finish line.

Pasta with the Rainbow

It's important to include protein at every meal. If you are a woman, you need about a palm size serving per meal. If you are a man, you need about two palm size servings. Many noodles have zero protein. Therefore, to ensure protein is consumed, meat is often added to pasta dishes. However, now there are many noodles made with beans which will give the meal some of that necessary protein. It is also important to eat the rainbow. You want to see a variety of colors on your plate at meal time. Each color has specific benefits to the body.

INGREDIENTS

Box of Lentil Pasta (it should list lentils alone as the ingredients)

1/2 cup broccoli

1/4 cup sliced red onion

1 red bell pepper

1 yellow bell pepper

1/2 cup shredded carrots

2 T olive oil

1/2 tsp Himalayan salt

2 cups water (to boil pasta)

PREPARATION

Boil water in a medium pot.

Add pasta to boiling water.

Lower to medium heat, and cook for about 8 minutes.

Heat olive oil over medium heat and add veggies.

Sauté until the veggies are tender.

Stir in the drained pasta.

Enjoy!

WHAT IS IT SERVING YOU?

Lentil pasta is rich in protein.

Red foods have lycopene and help protect the heart.

Orange and yellow foods have carotenoids which protect the skin, increase immunity, and support eye health.

Green foods are full of antioxidants.

Purple and blue foods have anti-aging as well as anti-inflammatory properties.

Stuffed Lentil Peppers

INGREDIENTS

1 whole red bell pepper

1 cup green lentils

1 cup gluten free brown rice or regular brown rice

1/4 cup spinach

3 T coconut oil

1 1/2 cup water

1 cup coconut milk

1/2 tsp Himalayan salt

1 clove garlic

PREPARATION

Heat the coconut oil in a medium saucepan. Add the onions and sauté for about 2 to 3 minutes. They should be translucent. Add the garlic and cook for an additional 2 minutes. Next, add your lentils and water. Bring to a rapid boil, lower and simmer for 20 to 25 minutes, or until lentils are tender.

While cooking the lentils, the brown rice should be cooking too. Place water, coconut milk, rice and Himalayan salt in a saucepan. Bring to boil and reduce heat. Simmer and cook for about 25 minutes.

Pour the cooked lentils and cooked rice into a large bowl. Mix together.

Time to add the mixed lentils, rice, and spinach into the gutted red bell pepper. This recipe is a great way to add a raw nutrient dense vegetable with something cooked. Raw foods are loaded with nutrient benefits and enzymes. It's good to have a mixture or raw and cooked food with your meal.

WHAT IS IT SERVING YOU?

Red bell peppers are packed with vitamin C. One medium red bell pepper serves your body 169% of the recommended daily intake (RDI) for vitamin C. It's been said to be one of the richest dietary sources of vitamin C and is a daily essential nutrient.

One cup of **lentils** will serve you 6.6 milligrams of iron. This means that you will already be at about 1/3 of your daily recommended amount. Having a sufficient amount of iron will keep oxygen pumping efficiently through the body

Brown rice helps contribute to strong and healthy bones because it is rich in calcium and magnesium. It also supports cardiovascular health because it contains selenium and is good for the heart.

Bursting Basil Lasagna

Many people just "cast" whatever ingredients they have on hand into a casserole hoping it lands and turns into a hearty meal they can serve more than one day. One of the most popular casserole type dishes is lasagna. While filled with ingredients many love, it's also filled with many ingredients that take away from the body's energy and cause the body to become very acidic. Remember, the PH balance of the body is of high importance. The meat, the cheese, the ricotta, the noodles all provide little nutritional value and are considered acidic to the body. Here's a lasagna that has a burst of body energizing ingredients. Always think "what can I add that's alkaline and what can I substitute that's acidic."

INGREDIENTS

1 cup of fresh basil

3 medium zucchini

3 medium squash

1 T flax meal + 2 tsps water

2 cloves garlic

8 oz. almond ricotta

1/3 cup nutritional yeast

1/4 cup fresh parsley

1/4 cup fresh oregano

1 box of gluten free pasta

3 cups water (to boil pasta)

Micro greens to garnish on top

2 jars of pasta sauce (low sodium or homemade sauce on page 98)

PREPARATION

Bring your water in a large pot to a boil. Next, add the noodles and reduce the heat to medium. Boil the noodles until tender. Once they are done, rinse in cool water until you are ready to use. To ensure the noodles don't stick add a half teaspoon of olive oil.

While the noodles are boiling, it's time to sauté the veggies. First, cut the zucchini and squash into round slices. Not too thin. In a small bowl, mix flax meal and water to make a flax egg.

In a medium saucepan, add 2 teaspoons of olive oil and increase to medium heat. Toss in the veggies and garlic. Sauté for about 2 minutes. You want to ensure that the veggies have a slight crunch as they'll be baking in the oven.

In a large bowl, mix the ricotta, parsley, oregano, nutritional yeast, and flax egg.

WHAT IS IT SERVING YOU?

Basil promotes a healthy gut and is good for depression.

Squash is rich in manganese and potassium.

Zucchini contains vitamin A, vitamin C, antioxidants.

FOR THE LAYERS

First is the pasta sauce.

Second are the noodles. One layer covering the sauce.

Third is the almond ricotta mixture. Spread evenly across the noodles.

Fourth is the FRESH basil. Be generous.

Fifth are the veggies (the zucchini and squash). Alternate each as you spread them across the basil. Repeat beginning with the first step. After following the layering sequence from the top, the last layer is the pasta sauce.

Preheat the oven to 325 degrees and cook for approximately 30 to 40 minutes.

Once cooked, allow the lasagna to cool and top with micro greens.

CollardGrin Wraps

A wrap is generally made with a huge flour tortilla circular shell. Many are so big that you can often find yourself eating more of the shell rather than the abundance of goodness inside. The moment I discovered using collard greens instead of the flour tortilla full of preservatives, the taste made me grin which is why I'm calling this recipe CollardGrin Wraps. The collard green is full of nutrient density and a fun way to bring life to your wraps.

INGREDIENTS

4 whole collard leaves

1 cup cooked brown rice

3 cups cilantro

1 lime, juiced

1 organic tomato, diced

1 avocado, cubed

Himalayan salt to taste

1 cup cooked black beans

1/4 onion, diced

1 clove garlic, minced

3 T olive oil

PREPARATION

Finely chop cilantro.

In a medium pot, add the water and rice. Bring to a boil, then lower to medium heat. Cook for 45 minutes until all the water is absorbed completely into the rice. Remove from heat and let cool. To the rice, add 2 cups finely copped cilantro, fresh lime juice, 2 tablespoons olive oil and himalayan salt. Mix well.

Rinse black beans well. Dice tomato.

In a bowl, add tomato, garlic, avocado, lime, onion, himalayan salt, 1 tablespoon olive oil, and cilantro. Mix well.

Heat rice and black beans in separate pans. Lay the whole collard green flat. The heat from the brown rice and the beans will blanch the collard.

Layer warmed brown rice and beans. Top generously with the tomato mixture from the bowl.

WHAT IS IT SERVING YOU?

Collard greens contain iron, vitamin C, vitamin K and calcium.
Brown rice has more fiber, antioxidants, and whole grains than white rice.
Cilantro is high in iron which helps with anemia.
Avocado is packed with potassium and essential fatty acids.
Black beans are agreat source of protein and are loaded with iron and magnesium.
Onion is high in vitamin, folate and vitamin B6.
Tomato is rich in vitamin A and vitamin K.

DINNER 94

The Crusty Cauliflower

INGREDIENTS

1 large head of cauliflower

2 T flaxmeal +
4 T water (flax egg)

3 T nutritional yeast

1 T fresh oregano

1 T fresh basil

3 cloves garlic

1 T arrow root

1/2 tsp himalayan salt

10 medium roma tomatoes

1 cup water

1/4 cup coconut sugar

2 tsp olive oil

1 T white vinegar

2 T garlic salt

PREPARATION

Preheat the oven to 375 degrees.

Grate the head of cauliflower until it is riced. Place water in a large pot and bring to a boil. Add the riced cauliflower. Cook for 5 to 7 minutes until cauliflower is soft. Once soft, drain with a fine mesh strainer and let cool. Use cheesecloth to drain any additional water. (This is important as you do not want the cauliflower to be watery.)

In a large bowl, add the flax meal and water. Stir well, and let sit for about 5 minutes until it changes consistency.

Next add cauliflower, flax egg, basil, oregano, arrowroot flour, nutritional yeast and himalayan salt. Stir until well combined. Taste and add seasonings, as needed.

Line a cooking sheet with parchment paper. Using your hands, make a dough ball and gently form into a round pizza shape and place on the cooking sheet.

For the pizza sauce: Place fresh tomatoes and olive oil in a blender. Blend on high until very smooth. In a large pot, pour the tomato sauce, fresh minced garlic, coconut sugar, and himalayan salt. Once cooled, transfer again to the blender and blend until smooth. Freeze additional sauce.

Cook the cauliflower crust without any toppings for about 45 minutes. Remove and flip to the other side. Cook for an additional 10 minutes. Remove crust from oven, and spread 2 to 3 tablespoons of sauce on cooked dough. Top with veggies of your choice. Bake for 10 more minutes.

WHAT IS IT SERVING YOU?

Cauliflower provides over 75% of the daily minimum target for vitamin C. It is also a cruciferous vegetable that contains natural substances that protect the branches and bends of blood vessels which are the areas most prone to inflammation. It is known as the health protectant vegetable.

The Saucy Black Pasta

INGREDIENTS

6 heirloom tomatoes

1 pack cherry tomatoes

1 red pepper

1 green pepper

6 cloves garlic, minced

1 large onion

1/3 cup minced fresh oregano

1/3 cup minced fresh basil

1 bay leaf

4 T olive oil

2 tsp coconut sugar

Himalayan salt

Italian seasoning

3 cups water (to boil pasta)

PREPARATION

Preheat oven to 375 degrees.

Cook lentil pasta according to package directions. Remove from heat and drain the water.

Cut heirloom tomatoes into cubes. Cut red pepper in half. Place tomatoes and red pepper on an 8 inch baking pan Drizzle two tablespoons of olive oil evenly over vegetables. Roast heirloom tomatoes and bell pepper for 15 to 20 minutes.

While the tomatoes and bell pepper are roasting, in a saucepan add olive oil, minced garlic, diced green bell pepper, diced onions, chopped fresh basil, chopped fresh oregano. Sauté for 3 to 5 minutes.

Remove items from the oven and let it cool.

Place roasted tomatoes and bell pepper in blender. Add veggies and sautéed herbs from saucepan. Add sugar and bay leaf to blender. Blend in the blender until desired consistency. Pour blended sauce in large saucepan.

In a food processor or blender, blend the cherry tomatoes keeping it chunky. Add the chunky tomatoes to the saucepan. Heat and season with himalayan salt to taste.

Pour over a lentil or whole grain pasta and enjoy.

WHAT IS IT SERVING YOU?

Heirloom tomatoes are rich in vitamin C and contain lycopene, one of the most powerful natural antioxidants. Lycopene has also been said to help the skin from harmful UV rays.

Porta~Bella Burgers

Burgers have become a handheld favorite for many years. Many people enjoy the taste and they require very little work to put together. It's not the production that requires effort, but the consumption that does. While your hands lift your juicy burger, your body gets ready to fight. It has to process a high amount of calories, saturated fat, cholesterol, sodium and more. It's time to think "beyond the burger." Food should work in your favor long after you have eaten it. This portobello burger will do just that. It will give you a burst of not just flavor, but favorable benefits for your body.

INGREDIENTS

4 portobello mushroom caps

3 T aged balsamic vinegar

1/2 tsp paprika

1/4 cup extra virgin olive oil

1 tsp liquid smoke

1/2 tsp Himalayan salt

1 tsp chili powder

1/4 cup fresh tarragon

PREPARATION

In a medium bowl mix the balsamic, paprika, extra virgin olive oil, himalayan salt, chili powder, and liquid smoke.

Add the portobello mushroom into the bowl and marinate for no less than one hour and up to eight.

Preheat oven to 400 degrees.

Top the marinated mushrooms with fresh tarragon. Bake the portobello mushrooms for 15 to 20 minutes mushroom cap-side down in the oven.

Put each portobello on a gluten free bun, top with the sauce, and add the toppings.

WHAT IS IT SERVING YOU

Many health experts call the **portobello** the "medicinal mushroom" due to its cancer fighting properties and immune boosting nutrients. It also serves you vitamin B-complex such as B2 (riboflavin) and B3 (niacin).

THE TOPPINGS

Top your burger with avocado, red cabbage, red onion, & spinach.

INGREDIENTS FOR THE TOPPING SAUCE

1/2 cup raw plain coconut yogurt

1 T fresh finely cut dill

2 T finely diced cucumbers without the skin

1 tsp lemon juice

2 cloves garlic, minced

1/2 tsp himalayan salt

PREPARATION

Combine all the ingredients, and let it sit in the fridge.

Sides

If you've ever been to a restaurant, then you've been asked that million dollar question, "what would you like for your side or sides?" The entree being the center of attention, and it's what many people think about first when ordering. Contrary to popular belief, the sides are just as important as the entree. So before you go with the popular choice of french fries, please remember that it's important your sides help to create an 80% alkaline to 20% acid combination on your plate. I broke down what's considered acid and alkaline in the previous chapter. When looking to increase energy and have a healthy pH of the body, the sides we choose matters. This chapter will provide some ideas to help energize those entrees.

The Cayenne Cold Buster

With many ailments in the body, food has the nutrient power to stop them in their tracks. Many people get what's called the "common cold". It's important to build up your body's immune system and defense. Colds tend to linger because of the build up of mucus in the body as well as inflammation. Quercetin, which is proven to shorten the symptoms of a cold, is found in many of the ingredients in this bowl. Take preventative measures during the cold season and understand that foods also provide healing to the body.

INGREDIENTS

2 large organic apples

1 small organic white onion

1 medium lemon, juiced

3 cups fresh organic spinach

1/2 tsp cayenne pepper

PREPARATION

With the skin left on the apple, cut it into small cubes after removing the core and place it in a salad bowl large enough to feed four people.

Cut the onion into cubes half the size of the apple cubes. Pour the onion into the bowl with the apples.

Squeeze lemon juice all over the salad.

Optional: Marinate the apples and onions in the refrigerator for at least one hour.

Toss in the lettuce.

Sprinkle cayenne pepper on top.

WHAT IS IT SERVING YOU?

Apples, onions, & spinach have quercetin which is a bioflavonoid that fights as an antioxidant to ward off colds.

Cool Cucumber Salad

INGREDIENTS

1 tsp sesame seeds

2 English cucumbers

1 red pepper

1 sweet onion

Himilayan salt to taste

1 T spicy sesame oil

1/2 to 2 inches peeled ginger

5 to 6 sprays of Amino Soy Sauce Alternative

2 tsp honey

1 lime, juiced

PREPARATION

Cut the cucumbers into squares.

Finely chop the red bell pepper.

Finely chop the sweet onion.

Put the cucumbers, bell pepper, and sweet onion in a large bowl.

Blend the sesame oil, ginger, honey, fresh lime, Bragg's amino, salt in a high power blender.

Pour the blended sauce into the bowl of cucumbers and veggies.

Mix together.

Sprinkle with black sesame seeds and cayenne pepper to finish.

WHAT IS IT SERVING YOU?

Cucumbers are high in vitamin K and have lots of water for hydration.

Red bell peppers have 300% of your daily vitamin C and are high in vitamin A which supports healthy eye sight. They are a great source of vitamin B6.

Ginger is anti-inflammatory, helps with digestion, reduces nausea.

The Big Dill Potato Salad

INGREDIENTS

6 to 8 red potatoes

1/4 cup chopped fresh dill

2 T olive oil

2 finely diced scallions

1 large lemon, juiced

2 tsp smoked paprika

Himalayan salt to taste

6 to 8 cups water

PREPARATION

Put the water in a large pot along with the unpeeled potatoes. Bring to a vigorous boil and simmer for about 15 more minutes until potatoes are tender and a fork can easily be inserted.

Remove from heat, drain water and let cool.

Once cooled, cut potatoes into squares leaving the red skin on them.

In a separate bowl, mix the lemon juice, smoked paprika, fresh dill, olive oil, and himalayan salt. Mix well and then add finely chopped scallions.

Pour mixture over the cut potatoes and toss until until all the potatoes are coated.

Place the potato salad in a radicchio bowl which should be eaten along with the potatoes salad.

Top with a sprinkle of smoked paprika.

WHAT IS IT SERVING YOU?

Red potatoes are high in fiber, B vitamins, iron, and potassium.

Fresh dill is high in fiber, calcium, riboflavin, and manganese.

Radicchio is a good source of selenium, calcium, vitamin K, vitamin C, vitamin A, Vitamin E, and folate.

Butternut Squash Vegan Mac & Cheese

Macaroni and cheese has been that comfort dish that is usually present at every major holiday function. Or that Sunday gathering or meal made with soul & love. One that everyone seems to enjoy. The traditional way however usually made with milk, cheese, & refined pasta. All ingredients that are acidic to the body contributing to weight gain, diabetes, and other ailments. This is a wonderful alternative that is meant to give you the taste you long and provide healthy benefits as well.

INGREDIENTS

1 medium Butternut squash

3 cups water

3 cups unsweetened almond milk or coconut milk

1 T coconut oil

3 T arrow root

4 T nutritional yeast

1 tsp ground dijon mustard

1/2 tsp onion powder

1/4 tsp Himalayan salt

1 tsp garlic powder

1/2 tsp dried oregano

1 tsp smoked paprika

1 box Lentil Pow Pasta

PREPARATION

Preheat the oven to 425 degrees.

Peel the squash and cut into cubes. Be sure to remove the seeds.

Toss the squash in the coconut oil and place back in pan for 30 to 40 minutes.

Bring 3 cups water to a boil and cook the lentil pasta.

In a sauce pan, add garlic, oregano until brown.

Add 2 cups almond milk or coconut milk, onion powder, arrow root, and wisk well ensuring no lumps. Next add, mustard, lemon juice, nutritional yeast, and stir until it thickens.

Once the squash is done and cools, add 1 cup of almond or coconut milk to a high powered blender and blend until smooth. Combine the ingredients from the sauce pan with the butternut squash purée and give it one last blend.

Reheat the sauce in the pan and pour over the lentil noodles.

WHAT IS IT SERVING YOU?

Butternut squash provides 100% of your vitamin A daily requirement, and is high in vitamin C & potassium.

Lentil Pow pasta is high in protein.

Kale Pico de GaYum

INGREDIENTS

1 bunch kale, minced

4 large tomatoes, small diced

2 red onions, small diced

2 jalapenos, seeded & small diced

1 cup cilantro minced

4 limes, juiced

2 T garlic powder

2 T paprika

2 T onion powder

Himalayan salt & pepper to taste

PREPARATION

In a large bowl, mix all ingredients and seasonings.

This recipe can very easily be turned into a wonderful guacamole. Just add 2 cups of kale pico to a bowl of 5 mashed avocados.

WHAT IS IT SERVING YOU?

Kale is high in two powerful antioxidants called quercetin and laempferol. It is also very high in vitamin A, vitamin K and vitamin C.

Tomatoes have substances called Lutein and Zeaxanthin that can help protect the eyes from the blue light from digital divices.

Red onions contain anthocyanins which helps to reduce heart disease.

Jalapeños contain vitamin B6 and vitamin C.

Pineapple Cilantro Brown Rice

Rice has become a dinner table staple for many around the world. Known for its ability to pair with protein and veggies in a noncompeting way, it simply just fits as a side filler. When asked which do you prefer, white or brown, many will say white. However, that is changing due to the knowledge of brown's healthier nutrient dense benefits. As we know, it's important to consume whole grains. White rice is not a whole grain, but brown rice is. Brown rice contains all parts of the grain, it contains the nutrient rich germ and the carb-rich endosperm while white rice is stripped of both. Brown rice is also high in fiber which is an essential part of your meals.

INGREDIENTS

1 cup brown rice

2 cups water

1/3 cup cilantro, finely chopped

1/2 cup pineapple, cubed

2/3 cup orange bell pepper, diced

2 tsps fresh lime juice

Himalayan salt to taste

PREPARATION

In a medium pot, add the rice and 2 cups water.

Bring to a boil and simmer on medium for about 30 minutes or until the rice is well done.

Allow to cool.

Once cooled stir in your finely chopped cilantro, cubed pineapples and orange bell pepper.

Sprinkle with lime.

Add himalayan salt to taste.

WHAT IS IT SERVING YOU?

Gluten free brown rice contains essential whole grains.

Pineapple is rich in vitamin C & manganese.

Orange bell pepper contains 190 percent of the recommended daily intake of vitamin C per serving.

Cilantro helps to rid the body from heavy metals such as cadmium, arsenic, lead, mercury, and aluminum.

Sweet Potato Fries

French fries are by far one of the world's best known foods. Held in your hand and dipped into the red sauce almost without thinking. It's become fast food's natural reflex (grab & dip). Many restaurants load your plate with them as a side for your burger or sandwich. However, it is not a simply "eat & digest" reflex for the body. The trans fat in fried potatoes raises the "bad," or LDL, cholesterol in the blood, which can lead to cardiovascular disease, obesity, and much more if consumed regularly. It also produces a chemical in the body called "acrylamide" when fried or baked on high heat. Acrylamide is toxic to the body. Why "fry" when you can free your body from the toxic chemicals and trans fats while still enjoying a grab & enjoy side item. Try these baked sweet potatoes. They are anti-inflammatory, high in potassium, have vitamin C & A, magnesium, and are a low glycemic food.

INGREDIENTS

4 to 5 sweet potatoes

2 tsps coconut oil

1 tsp cinnamon

1 tsp paprika

1 tsp himalayan salt

PREPARATION

Preheat oven to 300 degrees.

Peel and slice the sweet potatoes into sticks (not too thick).

In a separate bowl, mix the coconut oil, cinnamon, and paprika.

Toss the sweet potato sticks into the mixture and shake until evenly coated.

Lay without stacking on top of one another onto a baking sheet lined with parchment paper. Sprinkle evenly with salt.

Bake for 20 minutes at 300 degrees and then increase to 400 degrees for approximately 15 minutes to crisp.

WHAT IS IT SERVING YOU?

Sweet potatoes are anti-inflammatory, high in potassium, have vitamin C and A, magnesium, and are a low glycemic food.

The Watermelon & Cress Salad

INGREDIENTS

2 cups watermelon, cubed

1 cup watercress

1/3 cups fresh basil

1/3 cup fresh mint

1 fresh jalapeño

2 tsp olive oil

1/2 fresh lemon, juiced

1/2 fresh lime, juiced

Himilayan salt to taste

PREPARATION

In a large bowl, add the watercress. Cut watermelon into small cubes and add to bowl. Finely chop basil and fresh mint and add to bowl. Dice the jalapeños into small pieces and add to bowl. Drizzle the olive oil evenly. Squeeze the lemon and lime on top ensuring the seeds don't fall into the salad. Stir and add himalayan salt to taste.

WHAT IS IT SERVING YOU?

Watermelon contains citrulline and lycopene. Both are proven to help with cardiovascular health.

Watercress contains anticancer compounds.

Basil is an anti-inflammatory, improves blood flow, has vitamin K, and magnesium.

Mint inhibits the release of histamines that cause allergies.

Rosemary's Roasted Cabbage

INGREDIENTS

1 medium head of cabbage

1 pack of fresh rosemary

4 teaspoons olive oil

Himalayan salt to taste

PREPARATION

Cut the cabbage into an 1 ½ inch thick circles. Brush with olive oil on both sides. Sprinkle with a little himalayan salt. Top with fresh rosemary. Put on a baking sheet and roast for 20 minutes.

WHAT IS IT SERVING YOU?

Cabbage is among the top 10 sources that contain an important amino acid for the body called glutamine. It's an anti-inflammatory agent that helps with joint pain and arthritis.

Rosemary is considered a cognitive stimulant which can help with memory, alertness and focus.

Honest-to-Goodness Collards

I grew up watching collard greens being cooked with lots of meat. One of the common meats used was smoked turkey legs. I was told that it was to give it a good flavor. This healthy green has been known as a soul food staple at many meals like Thanksgiving, Christmas, family dinners, etc. However, when cooked with meat, it makes the collards acidic instead of keeping it's nutritious alkalinity. Here's a quick and easy recipe that will keep your collards flavorful but also more nutritious.

INGREDIENTS

Bushel of organic collards

1 clove garlic

3 tsp liquid smoke

1 small sweet onion

2 cups low sodium vegetable broth (or 2 cups of water)

Himalayan salt to taste

PREPARATION

Dice the onion. Chop the garlic into fine pieces. Wash collards thoroughly and cut into small strips.

Heat a large saucepan on medium heat and add the olive oil. Add the onions and garlic. Sauté the onions until translucent and tender. Add the greens and mix with the oil, onions, and garlic for 3 minutes. Then, add the low sodium vegetable broth (you can also substitute the broth for water), liquid smoke and himalayan salt.*

Cover and simmer on medium heat for 20 minutes.

*Please note that you may want to add additional salt to your liking.

WHAT IS IT SERVING YOU?

Collard greens are high in vitamin C, K, calcium, and loaded with potassium.

Onion contains chromium, which helps in controlling blood glucose and may be beneficial for preventing diabetes. Onions also have natural antibacterial properties known to help fight infection.

Garlic's antimicrobial, antifungal and antiviral properties help with the common cold and infections. It's been said that garlic is a preventative health agent that ranks second to turmeric.

121 SERVING YOU LIFE

Yummy Yucca Mash

INGREDIENTS

2 lbs yucca

3 garlic cloves, minced

1/2 tsp Himalayan salt

2 T vegan butter

1 cup no sugar added dairy free milk

5 to 7 cups water

PREPARATION

Peel yucca leaving no visible skin, and cut into square chunks. Place in large pot.

Add water to the pot, and ensure yucca is submerged with 1 inch of water covering them.

Add the garlic to the pot, and boil for 25 minutes or until yucca is tender.

Drain the water and put the yucca in a large mixing bowl. Add the milk, butter, and salt. Mix and whip until smooth.

WHAT IS IT SERVING YOU?

Yucca is also know as Cassava. It's full of vitamin C. It also stimulates the production of the white blood cells, which fight infections and viruses. It is also rich in B vitamins and high in potassium.

Classic Cabbage

INGREDIENTS

Small head of organic cabbage

1 small sweet onion

2 cloves of garlic, chopped

Himalayan salt to taste

2 tsp of olive oil

1 cup water

PREPARATION

Cut cabbage into long stredded slices.

In a medium saucepan heat the olive oil on medium heat.

Add the onion and garlic and stir for about 3 minutes until fragrant.

Add the cabbage and stir for 5 minutes until the olive oil is evenly coated.

Add 1 cup of water and simmer on low for 15 minutes. Season with himalayan salt to taste.

WHAT IS IT SERVING YOU?

Cooking cruciferous vegetables helps release indole, an organic compound that can fight off precancerous cells.

Zesty Asparagus

INGREDIENTS

1 large bunch of asparagus

2 tsp of olive oil

3 cloves of garlic

1 large lemon

1/2 tsp Himalayan salt

PREPARATION

Preheat oven to 350 degrees.

In a food processor or blender, add lemon juice, olive oil, and garlic cloves.

Pour liquid over the asparagus, and mix until the sauce coats the asparagus.

Lay the asparagus on a parchment paper lined baking sheet, and bake in the oven for 20 minutes.

WHAT IS IT SERVING YOU?

Asparagus contains vitamin A, C, K, fiber, & folate.

Kale & Apple Sauté

INGREDIENTS

1 package organic raw kale

1 apple, small diced

1/2 cup water

1 small sweet onion

2 tsp olive olive

Himalayan salt to taste

PREPARATION

Cut the kale or break it apart with your hands.

Finely dice half the onion, and wrap the other portion for a later dish.

In a medium saucepan, heat the olive oil using a medium temperature.

Add the onions and sauté for about 3 minutes.

Add the kale and stir for a minute.

Add the water and apples.

Allow to simmer for 5 to 7 minutes.

Season to taste with the himalayan salt.

Garnish with a few diced red bell peppers.

WHAT IS IT SERVING YOU?

Kale is a super green which scored high on the INDI chart for it's nutrient density, surpassing even spinach. It's high potency of vitamin A, K & C makes this leafy powerhouse green a nutritious dish or salad base for all. It's loaded with antioxidants that help remove free radicals from the body. It's important to buy organic kale because The Environmental Working Group listed kale as being a part of the "dirty dozen" which means if it's not grown organic, it's susceptible for contamination. Always wash your greens thoroughly!

Groovy Green Beans

INGREDIENTS

1 bag organic fresh green beans

1/2 cup raisins

2/3 cup slivered almonds

2 T olive oil

1/2 fresh lemon, juiced

1/2 tsp Himalayan salt

PREPARATION

In a medium saucepan, add the olive oil and heat on medium. Add the fresh green beans and sauté for 7 minutes or until tender. Squeeze in the lemon.

Add raisins, almonds, and himalayan salt. Stir for an additional 3 minutes.

Enjoy!

The Parsnipity Carrots

INGREDIENTS

5 to 6 carrots

5 to 6 parsnips

2 tsp of olive oil

1 T fresh thyme

Himalayan Salt to taste

PREPARATION

Preheat oven to 350 degrees.

Slice the carrots and parsnips and toss in olive oil.

Chop fresh thyme in fine pieces and add to the carrots, parsnips, and olive oil.

Add himalayan salt to taste.

Place on parchment paper lined baking sheet and roast 20 to 25 minutes in the oven.

Dressing Fit for a Holiday

Dressing is that holiday favorite along side that juicy piece of turkey. Many use sweet special occasions as that time to splurge. A plate stacked with so much food, you'll have to sit for hours just to let it settle. There are simple adjustments that we can make to those favorite recipes so we can still enjoy and make our holiday healthier.

INGREDIENTS

1 large sweet onion, diced

1/2 cup Fresh sage, chopped

Dried sage seasoning

2 cups gluten free cornmeal (be sure it's non-GMO)

2 cups gluten free all-purpose flour

2 cups low sodium vegetable stock

6 stalks celery, chopped

1/4 cup honey

3 tsp baking powder

1 tsp baking soda

2 T flax meal

2 tsps water

2 cups almond milk

PREPARATION

Preheat the oven to 400 degrees.

In a large mixing bowl mix cornmeal, baking soda, baking powder, honey, flour and almond milk. Pour mixture into pan and bake for 20 to 30 minutes. To check for doneness, insert a knife in to the dressing ensure it comes out clean. When done, remove from oven and let it cool.

In a medium saucepan, heat 2 tablespoons of olive oil over medium heat. Add onions and celery. Sauté for 3 to 4 minutes ensuring they don't burn. Add fresh sage and stir another minute and a half.

In a large bowl crumble the cooled cornbread with your hands. Add the onions, celery and fresh sage to the cornbread crumbles. Add the dried sage, black pepper, and vegetable stock. Stir until all the cornbread is evenly coated. Add more liquid, if needed but ensure it's not soupy.

Transfer the dressing into a well oiled baking dish. Cover with foil and bake for about 30 minutes. Uncover and bake for another 25 minutes until golden brown on top.

WHAT IS IT SERVING YOU?

Fresh sage has been known to lower blood glucose and cholesterol. It also contains many anti-inflammatory compounds said to be beneficial to our health.

Gluten free whole grain corn is rich in folate, B6, iron and has whole grains and selenium.

The Bold & Beautiful Brussels

INGREDIENTS

1 bag of organic brussels sprouts

2 T walnuts

2 T raisins

1 T olive oil

1 tsp pure maple syrup

1 tsp balsamic vinegar

1/2 tsp himalayan salt

PREPARATION

Preheat oven to 375 degrees.

Cut brussels sprouts into thirds and put into a bowl.

Add olive oil, pure maple syrup and balsamic vinegar. Mix until mixture is evenly coated onto the brussels sprouts.

Spread on a baking sheet lined with parchment paper and sprinkle with salt. Bake 15 minutes.

Remove from oven and sprinkle the walnuts and raisins and bake for 10 extra minutes.

WHAT IS IT SERVING YOU?

Brussels sprouts are rich in vitamin C and vitamin K. In 2008, there was a study that found that brussels sprouts could protect against carcinogens, or cancer-causing agents, and prevent oxidative damage to cells.

Sweet Acorn Adore

INGREDIENTS

1 medium acorn squash

2 T pure maple syrup

2 T walnuts, chopped

2 T coconut oil or vegan butter

1 tsp cinnamon

1 large apple, diced

PREPARATION

Preheat the oven to 350 degrees.

Cut the squash into two halfs, scoop out the seeds, and rinse.

Melt the butter (or use coconut oil). add the maple syrup, cinnamon. Add walnuts and apples to coat in the butter, then remove to a sheet of parchment paper.

Pour the remaining butter mixture over the squash and be sure to cover every inch.

Put the apples and walnuts in the open acorn cavity.

Drizzle with maple syrup and sprinkle with cinnamon.

Bake for 45 to 50 minutes.

WHAT IS IT SERVING YOU?

Acorn squash is high in vitamin C which gives your body that immunity boost needed to fight off the common cold & flu. One serving contains carotenoids that aid in fighting different cancers and illnesses. Known for its acorn shape, the acorn squash is one of the top 10 potassium-rich foods that's available for all to enjoy. They are also high in antioxidants.

The Chard-ged Rainbow

INGREDIENTS

1 bushel rainbow chard

2 cloves garlic

2 tsp olive oil

Himalayan salt to taste

1/2 red onion or sweet onion

1 jalapeño

2 tsps fresh lemon juice

2 tsp aged balsamic vinegar

PREPARATION

In a medium saucepan, heat the olive oil.

Saute the onions, garlic and jalapeno.

Add the Swiss chard and stir.

Add the balsamic and lemon.

Cook for 5 to 7 minutes.

Add himalayan salt to taste.

Serve and enjoy.

WHAT IS IT SERVING YOU?

Swiss Chard is a root vegetable loaded with vitamin K, A and C. It also contains potassium, fiber, magnesium, and iron.

Super Simple Lentils

INGREDIENTS

1 cup lentils

2 cups water

2 cloves garlic

1 small onion

2 T olive oil

1/2 tsp Himalayan salt to taste

PREPARATION

Rinse the lentils well in a mesh strainer.

Chop onions into fine pieces.

Mince or chop garlic into fine pieces.

In a medium saucepan, heat olive oil on medium. Pour the chopped onions and minced garlic into the pan. Sauté for about 3 to 5 minutes. Add the lentils and water. Bring to a vigorous boil, reduce heat to medium and cook for about 20 minutes until the lentils are tender.

Add himalayan salt to taste.

WHAT IS IT SERVING YOU?

Lentils are a complete protein and are high in fiber and iron.

Authentic Bahamas Peas & Rice

An Aunt Doretha Inspiration

As a tribute to my late father and mother, I wanted to include one of their favorite dishes. My father was born in the Bahamas and left when he was 10. However, he would take my siblings and I there on vacation during our childhood years which has continued through our adult years. What still amazes me about this beautiful island, is the amount of wellness at the fingertips of those that live there. Growing in their backyard are avocado trees, noni trees, fresh lemon grass, soursop, coconut trees, and much more. Another memory is this well known traditional rice dish with a healthier twist. It is my desire to help others around the globe discover more nutritious ways to make everyday dishes.

INGREDIENTS

3 cups organic basmati brown rice

4 cups water

2 T olive oil

1 1/2 medium onion

1 stalk celery, optional

1/2 medium (green) sweet pepper

2 ripe tomatoes, diced

2 cups green or dried peas, boiled

1/2 T sea salt, optional

PREPARATION

Sauté onion, sweet pepper, celery in olive oil for 2 minutes over medium heat.

Add tomatoes, sauté until blended.

Add water mix and boil for 5 minutes.

Add peas and seasoning, mix well and boil 10 minutes.

Add rice to boiling water, stir and reduce heat to low. Cook 30 mins or to package instructions.

🍃 WHAT IS IT SERVING YOU?

Pigeon peas are high in folate - a serving size provides 114% of the required folate amount for pregnant women. Peas are also high in fiber and protein.

Brown rice is packed with essential whole grains.

SIDES 140

Bahamas Coleslaw

An Aunt Doretha Inspiration

INGREDIENTS

2 cups shredded cabbage

1 cup shredded carrots

1 small onion, finely chopped

1/2 small green sweet pepper, finely chopped

1/2 red sweet pepper, finely chopped

2-3 T light vegannaise or natural organic dressing

1 T apple cider vinegar

1 T honey

PREPARATION

Combine shredded cabbage, carrots, onion and sweet green peppers.

Add mayonnaise/dressing, vinegar and honey.

Season to taste. Add a dash of sea salt or your choice of seasoning.

Toss and mix well.

Chill and serve on a bed of lettuce.

WHAT IS IT SERVING YOU?

Red & green cabbage contains vitamin C, K, B6, & folate.

A Sweet Delight

Since childhood, dessert has been a sweet part of many of our lives. "Eat all of your veggies and you'll get dessert," my parents would often say during my younger years. Now that I have a precious child of my own, I have the desire to serve him something delicious and decadent. I found a way to make it an extension a nutritious meal where both the veggies and dessert can contribute to the health of the body. So, my comment as a mother is, "eat your veggies and enjoy your dessert!" This chapter will satisfy your sweet tooth and increase your energy, too.

Chocolate PuCado

INGREDIENTS

2 ripe avocados

1/2 cup raw cacao

1/4 cup of pure maple syrup

1/4 cup almond milk

1 tsp vanilla extract (without alcohol)

PREPARATION

Peel and quarter a ripe avocado.

Put all the ingredients in a blender or food processor and blend until smooth.

Serve and enjoy!

Top with slivered almonds, blackberries, fresh coconut, and cacao nibs.

WHAT IS IT SERVING YOU?

Avocados contain the healthy fat that is loaded with vitamins and benefits. The healthy fat found in this creamy tasting vegetable is monounsaturated fat, which is also considered "good fat" and can reduce the level of bad cholesterol in your blood, lowering your risk of heart disease and stroke. It's also rich in potassium, vitamin K, B, C, & E.

Cacoa is a natural chocolate that comes from the seeds of the fruit of the cacao tree. It is a superfood that contains phytonutrients that help with mood, alertness, and mental clarity.It's also high in magnesium which is one of the most important minerals for the body. It helps relax the nerves, regulates blood pressure, and controls blood glucose levels.

Blackberries are abundant in vitamin C, vitamin A, and vitamin K.

The Sunshine Balls

Before you grab that protein bar or granola bar from the grocery store, consider making your own sunshine! There's a lot we can't control in life, but our food choices are up to us. Making your own bars cuts down on sugar and other additives that are not beneficial to the body. It's easy and your energy will shine!

INGREDIENTS

2 cups gluten free organic oats

1/2 cup flax meal

1/2 cup sunbutter

1/2 cup honey

Organic coconut shavings

*dark chocolate chips, optional

PREPARATION

Blend about 2 cups of oats the blender, until coarse powder forms.

Add the oat flour to a bowl. Next, add the flax meal, the sunbutter, and the honey. Mix well until it becomes a dough and very moist. Add the dark chocolate chips last. Scoop with a tablespoon into balls and slightly roll the balls over the coconut shavings.

Refrigerate overnight. If you prefer them cooked like in the picture, preheat the oven to 350 degrees. Bake for 15 minutes and let them cool. Enjoy either way!

Have fun with these and add ingredients that you like.

WHAT IS IT SERVING YOU?

Oats contain the soluble fiber, beta-glucan which slows digestion and increases satiety. They provide essential whole grains with compounds that help reduce inflammation and prevent heart disease.

Flax seeds ground into **flax meal** is a great way to add to recipes while reaping great benefits. Flax is one of the richest sources of omega-3 essential fatty acids. The body can't make them so we must get them from food. Flax is also proven to have antioxidant properties that help with breast cancer, reducing the size of tumors.

Sunbutter is made from nutrient dense sunflower seeds. For those that have nut allergies, sunbutter is a great way to enjoy that sandwich with homemade preserves or in a recipe like this one. Sunbutter is high in vitamin E as well as protein.

The Jolly Bean Brownie

It's nutrients in disguise.

INGREDIENTS

2 cups cooked black beans

1/3 cup dark chocolate chips

1/2 cup raw cacao

1/2 cup coconut flour

1/4 cup pure maple syrup

1 tsp baking powder

1/3 tsp pure vanilla extract (without alcohol)

2 tsp coconut oil

Flax egg: 2 tsp flax mixed in 6 tsp water

PREPARATION

Add the pure maple syrup, vanilla extract, coconut oil, and flax egg. Blend on high.

Add raw cacao, coconut flour, and baking powder. Blend on high until well blended.

Add the black beans and continue blending on high until everything is blended to perfection.

Pour the mixture in a medium bowl. Add the chocolate chips. Mix and pour into a greased baking pan.

Bake at 350 degrees for 35 to 40 minutes.

Let cool before serving.

Optional: Top with berries or a dairy free ice cream!

WHAT IS IT SERVING YOU?

Cacao powder is rich in magnesium and potassium

Black beans are high in protein and iron, help to maintain a strong bone structure, and are high in folate.

Dark Chocolate Lit Cookies

Keep your Energy Lit!

INGREDIENTS

1/2 cup almond flour

1/2 tsp baking powder

1/2 tsp baking soda

1 tsp pure vanilla extract

1/2 cup coconut sugar

1/8 cup almond milk

1/2 tsp Himalayan salt

3 T pure maple syrup

1 1/2 cups gluten free oats

2 T flax meal

2 tsp water

1 cup dark chocolate chips (62% cacao or higher)

1/3 cup coconut oil

PREPARATION

Preheat the oven to 350 degrees.

In a large bowl, mix the coconut oil, pure maple syrup, and coconut sugar until well blended. Add the almond milk and pure vanilla.

Make the flax egg by mixing the flax meal and water. Mix until you see the consistency change and become thicker. Add to the bowl and mix for 2 minutes.

In a high power blender, add the gluten free oats and blend until it's flour.

Add the almond flour and oat flour while continuing to mix. Add the baking powder, himalayan salt, and baking soda. Then, add the dark chocolate and mix slowly, keeping the chocolate in chunks.

Use a nonstick cooking sheet or line your baking dish with parchment paper.

Scoop dough into 1 inch balls and place 1/2 inch apart on a baking sheet.

Bake for about 15 minutes.

Remove, and let cool.

Enjoy with a cup of tea!

WHAT IS IT SERVING YOU?

A gluten free cookie with no refined sugars!

Oat flour is a whole grain. **Almond flour** contains protein. **Flax meal** contains omega-3 fatty acids and fiber. **Dark chocolate chips** are full of antioxidants.

The Coconut Berry

INGREDIENTS

1/2 cup blueberries

1/2 cup raspberries

2 T Coco Whip

1 T cacao nibs

PREPARATION

Layer with fresh raspberries and blueberries.

Top with Coco Whip, cacao nibs and sliced almonds (optional).

WHAT IS IT SERVING YOU?

Blueberries contain iron, calcium, magnesium and zinc.

Rasberries contian selenium, beta carotene and flavonoids.

Cacao nibs are high in fiber, magnesium and potassium.

ChocoLado Shake

INGREDIENTS

1 cup almond milk

1 frozen banana

1/2 frozen avocado

1/2 cup spinach

2 T cacoa powder

PREPARATION

Blend together in a high speed blender. Top with cacao nibs.

WHAT IS IT SERVING YOU?

Raw cacao is loaded with antioxidants. Its high source of magnesium causes the body to relax naturally. It boosts serotonin levels and helps lower blood pressure.

Bananas contain potassium, magnesium and fiber.

Avocados are packed with B vitamins and contain beta-sitosterol which helps maintain healthy cholesterol levels.

Spinach contains chlorophyll which helps to treat anemia and purifies the blood.

A SWEET DELIGHT

Sweet Potato Parfait

Sometimes, you may not have much time to spend in the kitchen making a pie. I'm all about spending less time in the kitchen and more time at the dinner table with your family or that special someone. You can still enjoy a decadent sweet potato delight without the crust.

INGREDIENTS

2 to 3 large sweet potatoes

1/4 cup coconut milk

3 T maple syrup

1 T pure vanilla extract

1/2 tsp cinnamon

2 tsps fresh squeezed orange juice

WHAT IS IT SERVING YOU?

Sweet potatoes are rich in vitamin A, fiber, and known to promote good gut health.

PREPARATION

Preheat oven to 400 degrees.

Wrap sweet potatoes in parchment paper and then place foil over the baking dish. Bake sweet potatoes for 45 minutes or until your fork easily glides through. The size will determine how long it will take to finish baking.*

Once baked, cut the sweet potatoes in half, scoop out the insides and put into the mixing bowl. If you prefer to let the potatoes cool, you will need to reheat the mixture in the oven or on the stovetop prior to serving.

Once all the sweet potato is removed from the skin and placed in the mixing bowl, it's time to add the additional ingredients. Add the pure maple syrup, vanilla, orange juice and cinnamon. Next, add the coconut milk. Use an emulsifier or electric mixer for a smoother texture.

Once mixed, it's time to layer!
The first layer is a scoop of warm sweet potato mixture.
The second layer is the walnuts.
The third layer is vegan Coco Whip or vegan vanilla ice cream.

Continue in that order and top with fresh coconut shavings.

*The sweet potatoes will be hot so put on mitts while handling them.

Baked Pear & Apple Crisp

INGREDIENTS

4 pears

4 apples

1 tsp pure vanilla

1 tsp raw ginger

1/2 tsp cinnamon

1/4 cup pure maple syrup or coconut sugar

1/4 cup vegan butter

1 tsp arrow root flour (optional)

PREPARATION

Preheat the oven to 375 degrees.

Core, peel and cut the pears and apples into cubes.

Purée ginger in a food processor.

Melt the butter and put in the vanilla, cinnamon, sugar, ginger, and arrowroot flour.

Stir on the stove for about a minute.

Toss in the cut pears and apples.

Spread in a 8x8 greased baking dish, and bake for about 30 to 40 minutes.

You don't need a crust or "crisp" for this dish. You can top it with some vegan whip, coconut ice cream, or homemade granola (see page 160). It's simple yet delightful!

WHAT IS IT SERVING YOU?

Apples and **pears** combined will serve you a dose of fiber needed to contribute to your daily requirements. Women need at least 25 grams of fiber per day while men need at least 38 grams per day. A pear will provide you 7.1 grams while that amazing crunchy apple will provide you 5.4 grams of fiber.

A SWEET DELIGHT 158

The Go-Getter Granola

Granola is wonderful as topping on a dessert, breakfast acai bowl, eating as cereal, or simply eating raw. Many over the counter bags of granola are full of sugar. This is an easy recipe that will still give you the taste and crunch you love.

INGREDIENTS

2 cups organic gluten free or regular oats

2 T coconut oil

1/4 cup honey

1 tsp vanilla

2 tsp chia seeds

1/4 cup fresh coconut

2 T pure maple syrup

PREPARATION

Preheat the oven to 350 degrees.

Add coconut oil to a medium saucepan and heat on medium. Then, add oats and lightly toast for 2 minutes until lightly golden Be sure not to let them burn or get too brown. Push the oats on one side of the pan and add the honey, vanilla, and maple syrup. Quickly stir the oats into the mixture in the pan until the oats are evenly coated. Remove from heat and add chia seeds and coconut.

Line a baking sheet with parchment paper. Spread the oats from the pan evenly onto the baking sheet. Toast in the oven for 8 minutes until they are golden brown. Remove and let cool.

WHAT IS IT SERVING YOU?

Oats are a great source of complex carbohydrates which provides sustainable energy during exercise.

Chia seeds are high in protein which helps build a stronger body, omega-3's, and fiber.

The Chocolaty Nut Cluster

INGREDIENTS

1/2 cup pure maple syrup

1 cup 100% raw cacao

1/2 cup 70% or higher dark chocolate chips

1/4 cup coconut oil

1 tsp pure vanilla

1 cup raw unsalted walnuts, raw unsalted sunflower seeds, brazil nuts or the nut of your choice! Just make sure it is not roasted or salted.

Coconut (optional)

PREPARATION

On low in a medium saucepan, pour in the coconut oil and the pure maple syrup. Melt together and then add the dark chocolate chips and the raw cacao. Stir until melted.

Stir in vanilla.

After the mixture has been stirred together for another minute. Remove from heat.

Put the nuts in a bowl and pour the chocolate mixture into the bowl. Stir until all the nuts are evenly coated.

Line a flat baking pan with parchment paper. Using a tablespoon, scoop the mixture an inch apart onto the pan. Put in the refrigerator for 3 to 4 hours until it gets hard. You can also put it in the freezer to reduce the amount of time to harden.

WHAT IS IT SERVING YOU?

Eating 2 pieces of **dark chocolate** with a content of 70% dark cacao or greater has been known to lower blood pressure and reduce hypertension. It's also rich in magnesium, fiber, and iron. Adding nuts gives you protein and takes the chocolate to another nutritious level.

Sit, Sip & Savor

Sometimes your digestive system needs a little break and smoothies, fresh juices, or something warm is a great way to give your body a rest while providing nutrients. Have a seat and raise a glass to your decision to add life-giving meals to your table by reading this cookbook.

Lemon Water with Melon

INGREDIENTS

3 lemon slices

1/2 cup honeydew melon and cantaloupe chunks

PREPARATION

Add melon and lemon slices to a Mason jar.

Fill with filtered water.

Refrigerate for an hour.

Consume within 24 hours.

WHAT IS IT SERVING YOU?

Vitamin C and **lemon juice** makes the water more alkaline.

Honeydew helps with healthy blood pressure levels and is rich in potassium. It also has a good amount of folate and vitamin K.

Cantaloupe provides 100% of the daily vitamin A requirements and 50% of the needed vitamin C per cup.

Coconut Water

INGREDIENTS

It's best to choose a **young coconut** instead of a mature one. When the coconut is young, it contains coconut water that is bursting with nutrients. When the coconut gets mature, the water turns into milk. The younger the coconut, the more nutritious the water inside. If you have ever seen pink coconut water, it's drained from a very young coconut. The pink water is full of flavor and benefits for the body.

PREPARATION

Carefully drill a hole in the shell and pour liquid into a glass. You can also use a hammer. Turn the coconut right side up and hammer until you see a few small cracks. Drain the water first and then continue to break apart to enjoy the nutty meat inside.

WHAT IS IT SERVING YOU?

Fresh coconut water is full of antioxidants and potassium. It is one of the most hydrating beverages that exists. Breaking into a real coconut releases a sweet nutrient dense enjoyment sure to tantalize your taste buds. In addition, you can enjoy the crunchy meat for a healthy snack.

Consuming coconut water from the source and not the shelf will give you optimal benefits from it's natural environment.

Ginger Tonic

INGREDIENTS

4 ounces peeled ginger root

6 to 7 cups sparkling mineral water

1/2 cup honey

1 fresh lime

PREPARATION

In a blender pour in the mineral water, honey, and ginger.

Blend on high.

Pour over ice or add ice to the blender and blend once more for a slushier drink.

Top with fresh mint.

WHAT IS IT SERVING YOU?

Ginger contains gingerol, which has powerful medicinal properties. Also known to help with chronic indigestion and menstrual pain.

Rosemary & Pineapple Water

INGREDIENTS

4 rosemary sprigs

1/2 cup pineapple chunks

Mason jar full of filtered water

PREPARATION

Add rosemary and pineapple to a Mason jar.

Fill with filtered water.

Refrigerate for 1 hour.

Will keep for 24 hours in the refrigerator.

WHAT IS IT SERVING YOU?

Rosemary is a natural relaxer easing stress and helping with circulation.

Pineapple helps with inflammation and is high in antioxidants.

Water with a Twist

Proper hydration is truly one of the most important parts of the day. It should always "come first before thirst". Once you're thirsty, more than likely, you've already reached some level of dehydration. Water pushes the toxins out of the body, repairs muscles, helps to disperse nutrients, aids in healthy digestion, and helps our organs to function properly. There's been much talk around the importance of drinking alkaline water which helps the PH of the body. It's also important to know that all water is not created equal. If you are purchasing water bottles from the store, please note that some brands are more acidic than others. Adding fresh lemon and lime to water increases the alkalinity. It's better to filter your own. However, if purchasing water in bottles, be sure that the plastic bottles say BPA (Bisphenol-A) free. BPA is a toxic chemical that lines many bottles and cans that's known to have dangerous affects on the body. It's best to filter your own and add ingredients that help to make your water more alkaline.

INGREDIENTS

1 lemon

1 lime

PREPARATION

Fill up a pitcher of water.

Wash lemon and lime.

Cut into circles and add to pitcher.

WHAT IS IT SERVING YOU?

Adding **lemon** to water helps to maintain the alkalinity and PH balance of the body. It also acts as detoxifying agent. Perfect to drink upon rising in the morning to get the digestive system moving.

The Fruit Waterfall

Naturally, we can get tired of just drinking plain water. Sometimes, you want that fruity and sweet taste. Instead of buying fruit punch and other beverages that are laced with sugar, it's best to make your own. You will have a waterfall of energy!

INGREDIENTS

1/2 cup strawberries

1/2 cup mango

1 small orange

1 lime

1 lemon

Amount of filtered water will depend on your pitcher. Use at least 4 cups of water.

PREPARATION

Add water to pitcher.

Cut lime, oranges, and lemons in round circles.

Add all fruits to the water.

Chill in the refrigerator and let the fruit infuse the water for 2 hours.

Pour and enjoy.

WHAT IS IT SERVING YOU?

A glass of fruity alkalinity and refreshment!

Get Juiced

There's nothing better than getting the juice from the source. Whether that's juicing your own oranges to get orange juice, or apples to get apple juice. When extracting the juice directly from the source, without processing or pasteurizing, you cut down on the sugar. In addition, fresh juicing provides more vitamins and antioxidants.

WATERMELON JUICE

Watermelon

Slice the watermelon and remove the seeds. Add the seedless chunks to the blender and blend on high. Pour the blended mixture into a mesh strainer. Add the smooth juice to a pitcher. Let chill in refrigerator and serve.

WHAT IS IT SERVING YOU?

Watermelon is rich in lycopene for heart health, is high in vitamin A, C, & potassium, and watermelon juice helps with onset muscle soreness.

THE GREEN LEAF*

During my career in nutrition, I've had many clients tell me that they don't like the texture of kale and other greens. My answer to that is to drink them until the tongue starts to like them. Juicing vegetables and fruits gives the digestive system a break from digesting fiber. For those that have an ailment, juicing will allow the body to absorb important vitamins and nutrients when eating is not the easiest option. A tall glass of fresh juice is bioavailable, meaning that it hits the system pretty quickly, serving the body goodness immediately. Juicing is also a great way to detox the body.

1 cup kale

1 cup spinach

1 cup dandelion greens

2 apples

1/2 lemon

Juice ingredients individually and stir together.

THE SOARING CELERY*

1 granny smith apple

3 stalks celery

5 carrots

1-inch piece fresh ginger, peeled

1/2 organic lemon

Add all ingredients to juicer. Let chill in refrigerator and serve.

WHAT IS IT SERVING YOU?

With the **celery** and **ginger**, this recipe will help to aid in healthy digestion.

*A juicer is required for this recipe.

Smoothie Body Bar

It can be smoothie happy hour any time of day! It's like having a meal in a glass. This is achieved once protein is added along with live foods such as fresh vegetables and fruits. A smoothie can also be a refreshing shake to satisfy that sweet craving. Whatever your choice, blending wholesome ingredients will give your digestive system a rest while still providing fiber for the body. If adding protein powder, it's important to ensure that it's clean. Some may contain traces of heavy metals, arsenic, preservatives, and added sugars. Therefore, it's important to do your research. Natural protein ingredients are nuts, seeds, and nut-butters. Cheers!

SWEET & SPICY SUNSHINE

1 cup coconut water

1/2 cup frozen mango

1 small banana, peeled, sliced and frozen

1 piece thumb-sized of fresh tumeric root, peeled

1 T freshly grated ginger

1/2 tsp cayenne pepper

1/2 tsp fresh lemon juice

CHOCOLATE PALM TREE

1 T cacao nibs

1/2 cup fresh coconut (raw is preferred)

1 cup coconut or almond milk

1 banana, peeled, sliced and frozen

SMOOTH NUTTY CHOCOLATE

1/2 avocado

1 cup spinach

1 banana, peeled, sliced and frozen

1 T cacao powder

2 T sun butter

1 cup almond milk or dairy free milk

THE YUMMY PERKY PUMPKIN

1/2 tsp nutmeg

1/2 cup fresh pumpkin puree

1 cup vanilla almond milk

1/2 cup ice

1/2 tsp cinnamon

1 banana, peeled, sliced and frozen

CHERRILICIOUS SMOOTHIE

1 cup frozen cherries

1 cup spinach

1 cup almond milk

3 T raw walnuts, chopped

1 tsp honey (optional)

STRAWBERRY SUNRISE

1/2 cup frozen strawberries

1 T chia seeds

1/2 cup frozen peaches

1 tsp flax meal

1 cup coconut milk

For a smoother blending experience, add the liquid first. Next, add the softer ingredients such as fresh vegetables (spinach), and fresh fruits. Add the harder ingredients last (frozen fruit, ice, and nuts).

Please note: be sure that your almond milk is carrageenan free. Carrageenan is an emulsifier used to thicken the milk that is a known carcinogen linked to cancer.

Warm It Up

HAUTE CHOCOLATE

Make it fancy, don't use a pack. You're far too haute.

1 cup almond milk

1 generous T cacao powder

2 tsps honey - sweeten to taste

Heat almond milk in a medium saucepan over medium heat. Almond milk heats up fast so be sure to watch it. Bring to a soft boil and add the cacao, stirring constantly for about 1 minute. Remove from heat and sweeten with honey to taste.

WHAT IS IT SERVING YOU?

Cacao is packed with magnesium, potassium, and even protein.

GET JAZZED WITH LEMONGRASS

1 long stem of lemongrass

2 cups hot water

1/2 slice fresh lemon

1 cube fresh ginger root

1 tsp honey - sweeten to taste

Cut lemongrass into 1/2 inch squares. Bring water to a boil. Place lemongrass and ginger in boiling water. Remove from heat. Squeeze lemon. Sweeten to taste with honey.

WHAT IS IT SERVING YOU?

Lemongrass helps to regulate blood pressure, is good for digestion, and is full of antioxidants.

TURMERIFIC TEA

Turmeric powder

1/2 sliced & peeled turmeric root

1/2 cup hot water

1/2 cup macadamia nut milk

1 tsp honey - sweeten to taste

1 tsp cinnamon

Heat the macadamia nut milk and hot water in a small sauce pan. Bring it to a simple boil and immediately simmer. Add the turmeric, honey, and cinnamon. Whisk until blended.

WHAT IS IT SERVING YOU?

Turmeric, also known as curcumin, is said to be an effective anitcarcinogen and known to have a substance that prevents certain illnesses. It is also serving you antioxidants known for their powerful anti-inflammory properties.

MINT FOR ME TEA

2 leaves fresh mint

1 tsp fresh lemon juice

1 cup hot water

1 tsp honey - sweeten to taste

Bring water to a boil. Add fresh mint leaves & lemon. Boil for 3 to 5 minutes. Let simmer and sweeten with honey.

WHAT IS IT SERVING YOU?

Mint has antibacterial and antiseptic properties that can aid in digestion. It also helps with an upset stomach. It's also anti-inflammatory and is said to improve brain function. Even if you are using a tea bag of your favorite flavor, adding fresh mint will serve will give you that healthy boost!

Schedule It Out

It's important to stay consistent with the times that you eat each day. According to dietary studies, it is suggested that we follow a regular eating schedule and by doing this it keeps the body operating like the incredible machine that it is. Eating the right balance of food consistently helps to maintain a healthy metabolism. This chapter will give you a small guide to help you schedule your meals. I hope you will eat consciously and with intention. Writing down your schedule is your vision of wellness.

Tanjie's Sample Eating Schedule

Your body is a beautiful machine and it requires the right fuel at specific times each day. To run your body at an optimal level, it's important to set and maintain a daily eating schedule. This will not only help to boost metabolism, but it will help to ensure that the right amount of nutrients are consumed throughout the day. If your eating is all over the place, this schedule should help you find balance and become more conscious about your consumption.

As soon as you wake up: Drink a glass of water or two with a little lemon.

Upon waking in the morning, consuming at least a full glass of water will help the body further push out toxins. This should enable you to excrete both in the form of urination and a bowel movement. It also jumpstarts the body since we are made up of about 60% of water. Consuming the proper amount of water per day ensures that nutrients are distributed throughout the body. Hydration also helps to maintain blood volume, improve liver and metabolic functions, and elevate fluid retention. Therefore, not only should you consume water first thing in the morning, but water should be consumed between each meal per the eating schedule below.

Breakfast (Example Time: 7am) – This meal should be eaten at least 30 minutes, and no later than an hour, after you wake up. Your body has been resting and it is ready to be fueled. This truly is the most important meal of the day.

Water (2 to 3 glasses of water) – During this time, your body is resting and digesting. You should not be eating anything during this time.

Small energizing mid-day meal (Example Time: 10am): This meal should be eaten between 2 to 3 hours after your breakfast.

Water (2 to 3 glasses of water) – During this time, your body is resting and digesting.

Lunch (Example Time: 12pm) – This meal should be eaten 2 to 3 hours after your mid-day energizing meal.

Water (2 to 3 glasses of water) – During this time, your body is resting and digesting.

Small energizing mid-afternoon meal (Example Time: 3pm): This meal should be eaten 2 to 3 hours after your lunch.

Water (2 to 3 glasses of water) – During this time, your body is resting and digesting.

Dinner (Example Time: 6pm) – This meal should be eaten 2 to 3 hours after your mid-afternoon energizing meal.

Water (2 to 3 glasses of water) – During this time, your body is resting and digesting.

Please note: Do your best not to eat after 7pm. If you usually eat very late start by moving the time up by an hour. For example, if you usually eat after 9pm, try not eating after 8pm until you eventually get to 7pm.

Weekly Meal Plan

Now that you've read about the importance of an eating schedule on the previous page, it's time to create one. In addition to your schedule, a plan of action concerning your meals will help you become more intentional. Your meal plan should include a serving of 6 to 8 vegetables and 3 to 5 servings of fruits per day. You should also ensure you have protein, grains, and healthy fats with your meal. Check your plate to see if you have a balance of 80% alkaline and 20% acidic foods. Also, there is a space to include your meal time. It's important to schedule it out and stick to it as best you can.

MEALS	SHOPPING LIST
Monday	
Breakfast time: __:__	
Mid-morning meal time: __:__	
Lunch time: __:__	
Mid-afternoon meal time: __:__	
Dinner time: __:__	
Tuesday	
Breakfast time: __:__	
Mid-morning meal time: __:__	
Lunch time: __:__	
Mid-afternoon meal time: __:__	
Dinner time: __:__	
Wednesday	
Breakfast time: __:__	
Mid-morning meal time: __:__	
Lunch time: __:__	
Mid-afternoon meal time: __:__	
Dinner time: __:__	

MEALS	SHOPPING LIST

Thursday

Breakfast time: ___:___

Mid-morning meal time: ___:___

Lunch time: ___:___

Mid-afternoon meal time: ___:___

Dinner time: ___:___

Friday

Breakfast time: ___:___

Mid-morning meal time: ___:___

Lunch time: ___:___

Mid-afternoon meal time: ___:___

Dinner time: ___:___

Saturday

Breakfast time: ___:___

Mid-morning meal time: ___:___

Lunch time: ___:___

Mid-afternoon meal time: ___:___

Dinner time: ___:___

Sunday

Breakfast time: ___:___

Mid-morning meal time: ___:___

Lunch time: ___:___

Mid-afternoon meal time: ___:___

Dinner time: ___:___

THANK YOU FOR TAKING THE TIME TO READ THIS COOKBOOK.

I hope you've been sharpened and ready to add more nutrient dense meals to your table. We are all the head chef of our kitchen not to mention our life. Live with intention and remember that wellness helps take you to your next dimension of greatness.

With life & love,

Tanjie Brewer

ABOUT THE AUTHOR

Over the years, Tanjie Brewer has been known for her client total body and life transformations. Her desire to see others rock their purpose with a lifestyle of vitality has been an inspiration around the globe. She is a Certified Nutrition Coach, Certified Personal Trainer, motivational speaker and wardrobe stylist. She believes that wellness must be intentional in order for life to be dimensional.

A SPECIAL "THANK YOU" TO MY TALENTED PHOTOGRAPHER! I ENJOYED MAKING THE DISHES AND SHE CAPTURED THE BEAUTY FOR YOU.

As a photographer, Joanne Xia developed a keen eye for details and colors. She loves to create imagery of portraits, food, and nature in a clean and editorial style. From conceptualization to execution to final imagery, she is devoted to capturing the inspirations and beauties from all around us.

www.ingramcontent.com/pod-product-compliance
Lightning Source LLC
Chambersburg PA
CBHW041151290426
44108CB00002B/39